AI Made Simple: Empowering Life After 55

Financial Management Handbook

Steve Munkeby

Title: AI Made Simple: Empowering Life After 55 –
Financial Management Handbook
Author: Dr. Steve Munkeby

Part of the AI Made Simple: Empowering Life After 55 Series
This book is one of ten in the *AI Made Simple: Empowering Life After 55* collection. Each book in the series is designed to stand alone and may be read in any order.

NextGen Publications, LLC
Website: https://SteveMunkeby.com
Email: drstevemunkeby@gmail.com
Phone: 470-302-4626

ISBNs:
Hardcover: 978-1-968702-04-5
Paperback: 978-1-968702-05-2
ebook: 978-1-968702-03-8

First Edition: June 2025
Printed in the United States of America

Cover Design: NextGen Publications, LLC
Interior Formatting: NextGen Publications, LLC

For more books and free resources, visit https://SteveMunkeby.com

Table of Contents

Foreword

In a rapidly changing world where technology continuously reshapes the way we live, work, and connect, people over 55 may feel either excluded from or overwhelmed by the rise of artificial intelligence (AI). The concept can seem daunting, the terminology complex, and the potential applications elusive. Yet, it's precisely this demographic – the experienced, resourceful, and insightful individuals often referred to as **older adults** – who stand to gain the most from the life-enhancing possibilities of AI. With this in mind, the collection of "*AI Made Simple - Empowering Life after 55*" **handbooks** (10 in all) have been carefully crafted to provide the accessible, practical guides to this transformative technology.

These 10 handbooks are more than an introduction to AI; they are a roadmap to empowerment. Written by a fellow older adult who understands the unique challenges and opportunities faced by those of us over 55, the handbooks seek to demystify AI and reveal its potential as a partner in creating a richer, more fulfilling life. Whether you are curious about exploring new hobbies, staying socially connected, or managing daily tasks with ease, these handbooks will show you how to harness the power of AI without the added confusion often associated with technology.

To ensure clarity and focus, the handbooks are organized into 10 distinct categories, each representing a specialized guide tailored to key areas where AI can enhance your quality of life. These categories have been thoughtfully selected to address a wide range of interests and needs, providing actionable insights, tools, and considerations for practical implementation. Together, they form a comprehensive resource designed to meet you where you are, empowering you to explore AI at your own pace and comfort level.

AI Handbook Collection: Your Guide to a Smarter Future

Each handbook offers an accessible introduction to the transformative power of AI in different aspects of life. Choose a book that aligns with your interests or needs and embark on an exciting journey into the world of artificial intelligence. Whether you select one or explore them all, these handbooks empower you to integrate AI seamlessly into your daily life.

---

1. Health and Wellness Handbook

Unlock AI-driven tools that are designed to enhance your overall well-being. From personalized fitness programs that adapt to your progress to AI-powered health monitoring that tracks vital signs and activity levels, these technologies help you stay active and informed. Explore virtual health consultations for remote medical advice, AI-driven nutrition tools for meal planning, and mental health chatbots for emotional support. Whether you're managing a chronic condition or optimizing your wellness routine, AI is here to support your journey.

---

2. Companionship and Mental Health Handbook

Combat loneliness and boost emotional well-being with AI-powered virtual companions, mindfulness applications, and intelligent therapy tools. These AI-driven solutions offer real-time conversations, guided meditation sessions, and mood tracking to support mental wellness. Whether you seek casual companionship through chatbots or structured therapy through AI-driven counseling tools, this handbook helps you harness technology to build emotional resilience and maintain a positive mindset.

---

3. Financial Management Handbook

Navigate your finances with confidence using AI-powered tools that simplify budgeting, track spending, and provide smart investment insights. AI-powered financial assistants help manage expenses, fraud detection systems protect your accounts, and retirement planning tools offer projections for future security. Learn how AI can help you automate bill payments, optimize savings plans, and even provide personalized financial coaching, ensuring that you stay in control of your financial future.

---

4. Learning and Personal Development Handbook

Embrace lifelong learning with AI-powered education platforms, language translation tools, and creative AI applications that expand your knowledge. Whether you want to learn a new language, improve professional skills, or explore creative outlets like music composition or writing, AI provides tailored learning paths that adapt to your pace. Engage with personalized tutors, immersive virtual classrooms, and interactive learning modules that make acquiring new skills engaging and efficient.

5. Memory and Cognitive Training Handbook

Keep your mind sharp and active with AI-driven brain-training games, memory enhancement tools, and cognitive exercises designed to boost mental agility. AI-powered tools can help you track memory patterns, stimulate problem-solving skills, and even provide early detection for cognitive decline. Whether you're looking to enhance your focus, improve recall, or simply stay mentally engaged, AI solutions offer personalized routines that make cognitive health a daily priority.

6. Hobbies and Entertainment Handbook

Enhance your leisure time with AI-powered tools that cater to your favorite hobbies. Discover AI-generated art and music tools, smart gardening assistants, photography enhancement tools, and gaming experiences tailored to your preferences. AI can also recommend movies, books, and activities based on your interests, ensuring that your downtime is always enjoyable and inspiring. Whether you're exploring a new passion or deepening an existing one, AI can guide and enrich your hobby experience.

7. Communication and Connection Handbook

Stay connected with family, friends, and the world using AI-enhanced communication tools. AI-powered voice-to-text tools, smart video calling platforms, and real-time translation services break down language barriers and make interactions more accessible. Whether you're enhancing digital conversations, staying in touch with distant loved ones, or navigating a new language, AI-driven solutions simplify communication and strengthen your connections.

---

8. Home and Daily Living Handbook

Make daily life more convenient with AI-powered smart home automation, virtual assistants, and organizational tools. Learn how AI can simplify grocery shopping, streamline household management, and even provide reminders for medication or important appointments. Whether you want to automate home security, adjust smart lighting, or use AI for meal planning, this handbook provides practical solutions to make everyday tasks effortless.

---

9. Accessibility Handbook

Empower yourself with AI solutions that enhance independence and accessibility. Discover AI-driven screen readers, real-time text-to-speech applications, voice-activated assistants, and mobility aids that break down barriers for people with disabilities. These technologies improve navigation, enhance communication, and provide greater control over your environment, ensuring that AI serves as a bridge to a more inclusive and accessible world.

---

10. Travel and Exploration Handbook

Travel is smarter with AI-powered trip planners, virtual travel experiences, and language translation tools that make navigating the world easier. AI can help find the best travel deals, create personalized itineraries, and offer real-time navigation assistance. Whether you're planning a trip abroad, exploring new cities, or experiencing virtual tourism from home, AI enhances the way you discover and engage with the world.

Start Your AI Journey Today!

Each handbook serves as a gateway to understanding and integrating AI into different aspects of life. Choose the one that speaks to your needs and start experiencing the benefits of AI today!

The beauty of AI lies in its versatility and capacity to be tailored to older adult preferences and abilities. Unlike one-size-fits-all solutions, AI adapts to your specific circumstances, enabling you to achieve goals that might otherwise seem out of reach. For instance, an AI companion tool can help you stay organized by setting reminders and managing your calendar, while an AI-driven creative tool can inspire you to write poetry or design greeting cards for friends and family. These innovations are not just conveniences; they represent opportunities for personal growth, creativity, and connection.

As someone who shares this stage of life with you, I understand the concerns and reservations felt when approaching new technology.

It's natural to wonder whether it's worth the effort to learn, whether it will truly improve your life, or whether it might create new frustrations. These are valid questions, and they deserve thoughtful answers. Through these handbooks, my goal is to address these concerns head-on, providing reassurance, clear explanations, and step-by-step guidance to help you confidently embrace AI. You will find real-world examples, practical tips, and relatable scenarios that make the concepts not only understandable but also engaging and enjoyable.

Moreover, these handbooks emphasize the importance of maintaining a sense of control and balance in adopting AI. Technology should serve as a tool to enhance your life, not as a source of dependency or stress. To that end, we will explore how to set boundaries, prioritize what matters most, and use AI in a way that aligns with our values and goals. By approaching AI with curiosity and intentionality, you can harness its potential to empower, rather than overwhelm, your journey.

The "*AI Made Simple - Empowering Life after 55*" handbooks are not just a guide; they are an invitation to a new chapter of possibility. Each handbook is a reminder that learning and growth do not have an expiration date, and that technology, when approached with the right mindset, can be a powerful ally in achieving a vibrant and fulfilling life. Whether you are taking your first tentative steps into the world of AI or looking to deepen your understanding within a specific category that a handbook addresses, each handbook offers a supportive companion to guide you along the way.

In closing, I want to thank you for choosing this journey and for embracing the spirit of exploration that has brought you to these pages. As you delve into one or all of the 10 handbooks and discover the ways AI can enrich your life, I encourage you to approach each chapter of each handbook with an open mind and a sense of adventure. The road ahead is filled with opportunities to learn, connect, and grow—and I am honored to walk it with you.

Welcome to the "*AI Made Simple - Empowering Life after 55*" handbook collection! Let us embark on this journey together, transforming what once seemed complex into a source of empowerment, joy, and discovery.

Introduction

The Search for Clear Answers and a Trusted Friend in Technology

For older adults, the fast-paced changes in technology can feel overwhelming. Finding someone to talk to about personal challenges or complex topics can also be difficult. In the past, magazines and newspapers were the main sources of reliable information. You could turn a page, read an article, and feel confident about what you learned. But today, most information is found online. While the internet offers an endless supply of information, it's not always easy to find the facts you need.

Online content often includes countless opinions and contradictory viewpoints, making it hard to understand what is true or useful. This complexity can leave you feeling lost. **What you need is a trusted friend,** someone who can listen to your questions, explain things simply, and guide you to the right answers. That trusted friend can be found in artificial intelligence (AI).

What Is Artificial Intelligence?

Artificial intelligence, often shortened to AI, is a type of technology that can think, learn, and answer questions in ways that seem very smart. The word "artificial" is used because the intelligence does not come from a real person. Instead, it comes from a computer system. When you ask a question, AI gathers information from computers around the world. It sifts through millions of pieces of information and simplifies it into a clear answer, similar to what a knowledgeable friend might do. While it might seem like talking to a real person, the answers come from an intelligent computer program designed to imitate human understanding.

Meet Your New Smart Friend: ChatGPT

One of the most popular and helpful AI tools is called ChatGPT. The "GPT" stands for "Generative Pre-trained Transformer." While that may sound complicated, what is important to know is that ChatGPT is designed to have conversations with you. It listens to your questions, understands them, and provides easy-to-understand answers. ChatGPT is a type of AI known as generative AI, which means it can create responses, explanations, and even new ideas based on what you ask.

What Is Generative AI?

Generative AI refers to artificial intelligence tools that can create new content. This includes written text, images, music, and more. Unlike traditional tools that only provide pre-set answers, generative AI can create fresh ideas and explanations, tailored to your specific questions. ChatGPT is one of the best examples of this technology. It's designed to "talk" with you in a conversational style, making it feel natural and easy to use.

Why Should Older Adults Care About ChatGPT and Generative AI?

For older adults, ChatGPT and generative AI can be life-changing tools. They help simplify modern technology and provide a new way to access information, learn, and solve problems. Here are the key reasons why it's worth understanding:

- **Answers Without Judgment**: You can ask ChatGPT anything, no matter how simple or complicated, without worrying about being judged. It's like having a patient, knowledgeable tutor available 24/7.
- **Simplifying Complex Topics**: Whether it's understanding medical reports, fixing a computer issue, or learning about a new hobby, ChatGPT can break down complex topics into plain, understandable language.
- **Convenience**: Instead of sifting through countless websites and articles, ChatGPT brings the answers directly to you in seconds.
- **Confidence**: When you use ChatGPT, you can feel more confident understanding new things, staying informed, and making decisions.
- **Staying Connected**: ChatGPT can help you keep up with the latest trends, whether it's understanding popular topics, learning how to use tools, or even crafting thoughtful messages to friends and family.

What Do You Need to Use ChatGPT?

Getting started with ChatGPT is easier than you might think. Here is what you will need:

- **A Device with Internet Access**: This could be a smartphone, tablet, or computer. For the best experience, a computer with internet access is recommended.

- **A Subscription to ChatGPT**: Select versions of ChatGPT are free, while others offer additional features for a small monthly fee. Choose the one that fits your needs. (Type the following into a web search on your device – "How do I obtain a subscription to ChatGPT")
- **Basic Copy-and-Paste Skills**: Sometimes, you might want to copy information from an email, website, or document to share with ChatGPT. If you are not familiar with copying and pasting, do not worry, it's a simple skill that you can learn quickly. YouTube has examples for learning this skill. (Type the following into a web search on your device – "YouTube – How to copy and paste for beginners")
- **Questions to Ask**: You can ask ChatGPT anything. Whether you need help understanding something you have read, solving a problem, or exploring a new topic, just type your question into the ChatGPT interface and wait for its response. (Type the following into a web search on your device – "YouTube – What does ChatGPT interface look like")

How ChatGPT Works for You

Imagine you are trying to understand a complicated health report from your doctor. Instead of struggling to make sense of the medical jargon, you can copy the text and paste it into ChatGPT. You could then ask, "Can you explain the provided information in simple terms?" Within moments, ChatGPT will provide a clear, straightforward explanation.

If you are planning a trip and need help figuring out the best time to visit a destination, you could ask ChatGPT, "What is the best time of year to visit Paris?" ChatGPT will consider weather, events, and other factors to give you a helpful answer.

Practical Uses for ChatGPT

ChatGPT can make life easier for older adults by addressing practical uses of AI:

Personalized Health Monitoring

Generative AI enables a new level of precision in health tracking and management:

- **AI-Powered Wearables:** Devices like smartwatches monitor vital signs, physical activity, and sleep patterns around the clock. These wearables provide actionable insights by analyzing real-time data.
- **Predictive Analysis:** AI tools analyze trends in health data to identify early warning signs of issues such as heart disease or diabetes, allowing for timely interventions.
- **Tailored Recommendations:** Based on your unique health profile, AI suggests lifestyle adjustments, like increasing physical activity or improving sleep hygiene, to keep you at your best.

Medication Management

Managing medications becomes easier and safer with AI-powered systems:

- **Personalized Schedules:** Generative AI creates medication plans customized to your prescriptions and medical history, ensuring accuracy and adherence.
- **Reminders and Alerts:** These tools send reminders to take medications at the right time and warn you of potential drug interactions.
- **Voice-Activated Assistance:** Virtual assistants, like smart speakers, answer questions about medication use, making it simple to stay informed.

Cognitive Support

AI helps older adults maintain sharp minds and manage cognitive challenges:

- **Custom Exercises:** AI designs engaging brain-training activities based on your interests and cognitive needs, improving memory and focus.
- **Memory Aids:** Tools like virtual calendars and to-do lists help organize daily tasks, reducing stress and enhancing independence.
- **Cognitive Decline Management:** Generative AI supports older adults experiencing early signs of cognitive decline by adapting tools to their specific needs.

Emotional and Mental Health

Generative AI fosters emotional well-being and combats loneliness:

- **Companionship:** AI-powered chatbots provide meaningful conversations and emotional support, reducing feelings of isolation.
- **Mental Health Monitoring:** AI can analyze speech patterns and emotional cues to detect early signs of anxiety or depression, recommending tailored self-care activities or professional help.
- **Stress Relief Tools:** From guided meditation to calming music, AI offers a variety of options to manage stress and improve mood.

Fitness and Nutrition Guidance

AI transforms staying healthy into a personalized experience:

- **Fitness Tracking:** Smart devices monitor activity levels and suggest exercises suited to your mobility and fitness goals.
- **Real-Time Feedback:** During workouts, AI provides immediate tips to improve form and prevent injury.
- **Customized Meal Plans:** AI designs meal plans based on your dietary preferences and health needs, offering grocery lists and recipes that make healthy eating simple.

Enhancing Accessibility

Generative AI improves mobility and access to essential services:

- **Smart Home Integration:** AI-enabled devices respond to voice commands, allowing you to control lights, appliances, and security systems with ease.
- **Assistive Technologies:** Innovations like robotic walkers and voice-controlled wheelchairs support mobility and independence.
- **Information Accessibility:** AI tools transcribe and summarize medical consultations, ensuring you understand and retain critical health information.

Bridging the Digital Divide

AI simplifies technology, making it more accessible to older adults:

- **Intuitive Interfaces:** User-friendly designs and conversational AI reduce barriers to adopting new technologies.
- **Learning Tools:** AI-based tutorials teach older adults how to navigate smartphones, tools, and online platforms confidently.

And Away We Go!

For older adults, ChatGPT and generative AI open up a world of possibilities. ChatGPT and AI make it easier to learn, stay informed, and manage daily challenges without feeling left behind by technology. **Think of ChatGPT as your new smart friend**, always ready to help, explain, and guide you through life's questions with patience and clarity.

The best part? Getting started is simple, and the benefits are endless. Whether you are curious about something new, need help solving a problem, or just want to learn more about the world, AI and ChatGPT are available to help with knowledge and insights.

To fully embrace the benefits of generative AI, older adults must approach these tools with curiosity and an open mind. The journey toward improved **health and wellness** isn't only about technological advancement but also about personal growth and adaptability. By integrating AI into daily life, the opportunities for enhanced living in later years are boundless.

Financial Management

Introduction

Financial management is a fundamental aspect of life at any age, but for older adults, it takes on heightened significance. As older adults navigate the complexities of retirement planning, healthcare costs, estate management, and maintaining financial independence, the need for effective financial strategies becomes indispensable. A well-structured financial plan not only ensures a comfortable and secure lifestyle but also provides peace of mind, allowing older adults to focus on enjoying life and pursuing their passions without financial stress.

In recent years, generative artificial intelligence (AI) has emerged as a transformative force in financial management. AI-powered tools offer insights, automation, and real-time financial recommendations that empower older adults to make informed decisions, manage risks, and optimize their financial resources. These advanced technologies simplify financial tasks, enhance security, and provide personalized solutions tailored to older adult needs.

This handbook explores the concept of financial management, examines the unique challenges older adults face, highlights the potential of generative AI, and outlines essential skills older adults need to harness AI-driven financial tools effectively.

Defining Financial Management

Financial management refers to the strategic process of planning, organizing, controlling, and monitoring financial resources to achieve stability and long-term financial goals. For older adults, financial management becomes even more critical as they navigate life transitions such as retirement, rising healthcare expenses, and estate planning.

Key Aspects of Financial Management for Older Adults

- **Budgeting:** Establishing a comprehensive budget that accounts for fixed income sources such as Social Security, pensions, retirement savings, and annuities while managing expenses to sustain a comfortable lifestyle.
- **Investment Planning:** Ensuring continued financial growth by adopting prudent investment strategies that balance risk and return based on retirement timelines and income needs.
- **Retirement Planning:** Securing a financially stable retirement by optimizing savings, maximizing Social Security benefits, and exploring annuities or other income-generating options.
- **Healthcare Cost Management:** Preparing for increasing medical expenses, including insurance premiums, long-term care, prescription medications, and unexpected medical emergencies.
- **Estate and Legacy Planning:** Structuring asset distribution to ensure financial security for beneficiaries, support charitable causes, and minimize estate taxes.

The Importance of Financial Management

Effective financial management allows older adults to maintain financial independence, meet obligations, and provide for their loved ones. It also:

- **Reduces financial stress:** A well-organized financial plan minimizes uncertainty and anxiety about future expenses.
- **Ensures sustainability of resources:** Proper planning helps prevent financial depletion and ensures financial security throughout retirement.
- **Enhances financial security:** Strategic decision-making safeguards against inflation, economic downturns, and unexpected expenses.
- **Facilitates informed decision-making:** A deep understanding of financial options and strategies empowers older adults to make choices that align with their long-term goals.

Challenges in Financial Management for Older Adults

Aging introduces unique financial challenges that require careful planning and proactive strategies. Below are common financial hurdles older adults face:

Declining Income

- Transitioning from a steady income to fixed retirement funds limits financial flexibility.

- Adjusting spending habits to match a reduced income can be challenging.
- Inflation erodes purchasing power, necessitating financial adjustments to sustain living standards.

Rising Healthcare Costs

- Medical expenses, including insurance premiums, prescription drugs, and long-term care, increase significantly with age.
- Chronic illnesses and unexpected medical emergencies can create substantial financial strain.
- Long-term care services, such as nursing homes and home healthcare, add further financial burdens.

Longevity Risk

- Older adults may outlive their financial plans, increasing the risk of exhausting savings.
- Market fluctuations and economic downturns can affect retirement funds and investment portfolios.
- Rising costs of living require long-term adaptability and financial foresight.

Financial Fraud and Scams

- Older adults are frequently targeted by scams, including phishing emails, fraudulent investment schemes, and identity theft.
- Lack of familiarity with modern digital security practices heightens vulnerability.
- Cognitive decline can make older adults more susceptible to financial exploitation.

Complex Financial Products

- Understanding financial instruments such as annuities, insurance policies, and investment options can be overwhelming.
- Misinterpretation of financial products can lead to poor financial decisions and financial losses.
- Choosing between different retirement withdrawal strategies requires financial literacy and guidance.

Technological Barriers

- Modern financial tools and platforms require digital proficiency, which older adults may lack.
- Online banking, budgeting apps, and investment platforms can be difficult to navigate without assistance.
- A lack of accessible, older adult-friendly financial tools can hinder effective financial management.

The Role of Generative AI in Financial Management

Generative AI is reshaping financial management for older adults by providing intelligent, data-driven solutions that address common financial challenges. Here's how AI can assist:

Personalized Financial Planning

- AI-driven tools analyze income, expenses, and financial goals to create customized financial plans.

- Predictive modeling simulates various financial scenarios, helping older adults prepare for different economic conditions.

Expense Tracking and Budgeting

- AI-powered applications automatically track spending, categorize expenses, and generate real-time financial insights.
- Automated alerts notify older adults about overspending, bill due dates, and potential fraudulent transactions.

Investment Advice

- AI algorithms provide investment recommendations tailored to older adult's risk tolerance and financial goals.
- Continuous monitoring and AI-driven portfolio rebalancing optimize returns and mitigate risks.

Fraud Detection and Security

- AI-powered security systems detect suspicious financial activities and alert older adults or their trusted contacts.
- Advanced authentication methods, including biometric security, enhance financial safety.

Simplifying Complex Financial Products

- AI tools break down complicated financial concepts into easy-to-understand explanations.
- Virtual assistants and chatbots guide users through investment decisions, insurance policies, and estate planning.

Tax Planning

- AI-driven tax software analyzes income, deductions, and credits to optimize tax efficiency.
- Automated tax compliance systems reduce filing errors and ensure adherence to regulations.

Healthcare Expense Management

- AI applications predict future healthcare costs based on medical history and inflation trends.
- Cost-comparison tools help older adults select affordable insurance plans and identify savings on prescription drugs.

Financial management is a crucial component of life after retirement, encompassing budgeting, investment planning, healthcare expense management, and estate organization. While older adults face significant financial challenges, including declining income, rising medical costs, and vulnerability to scams, generative AI offers innovative solutions that simplify financial decision-making and enhance financial security.

By integrating AI-powered financial tools into their daily routines, older adults can gain greater control over their finances, mitigate risks, and improve their overall quality of life. However, to fully leverage these advancements, embracing digital literacy and financial education is essential. With the right tools, knowledge, and guidance, older adults can confidently navigate their financial futures, ensuring stability, security, and peace of mind throughout retirement.

The journey toward harnessing generative AI is as much about personal growth as it's about technological advancement. The following 10 chapters delve deeper into specific **financial management** tools and strategies to make this vision a reality.

Chapter 1: Budgeting Assistance

AI-powered budgeting tools streamline financial planning by automatically categorizing income and expenses. These tools use machine learning algorithms to analyze spending patterns, helping older adults track their finances effortlessly. With visual dashboards, older adults can gain clear insights into their financial health, ensuring they remain within budget.

Over time, AI systems adapt to user behavior, offering personalized recommendations on cost-saving measures. For instance, they can alert users to recurring subscriptions they no longer use or suggest lower-cost alternatives for common expenses. AI tools even allow users to set financial goals, while providing step-by-step guidance on how to achieve them.

By integrating AI into budgeting, older adults can eliminate the stress of manual expense tracking, focus on optimizing their resources, and maintain financial stability in retirement.

Chapter 2: Fraud Detection

Financial fraud is a growing concern, particularly for older adults who may be more vulnerable to scams. AI-driven fraud detection tools provide an extra layer of security by monitoring financial transactions in real-time. These systems analyze patterns and flag suspicious activities, such as unauthorized transactions or phishing attempts.

Advanced fraud detection algorithms can detect inconsistencies in spending behavior and immediately notify users of potential threats. AI tools may integrate biometric authentication for enhanced security, reducing the risk of identity theft. Additionally, virtual assistants can educate older adults on common financial scams and provide real-time guidance when suspicious activities arise.

By leveraging AI for fraud detection, older adults can safeguard their finances, minimize risks, and enjoy peace of mind knowing their accounts are protected.

Chapter 3: Investment Advice

Investing can be overwhelming, especially for older adults unfamiliar with financial markets. AI-powered investment platforms simplify this process by offering personalized recommendations based on financial goals, risk tolerance, and market conditions.

These tools analyze vast amounts of financial data to provide tailored investment strategies. They can suggest diversified portfolios, automate rebalancing, and even predict market trends using predictive analytics. AI-driven financial advisors, also known as robo-advisors, offer cost-effective investment management, eliminating the need for expensive human advisors.

With AI-driven investment tools, older adults can confidently grow their wealth while minimizing risks and maintaining control over their financial future.

Chapter 4: Retirement Planning

AI-based retirement planning tools evaluate an older adult's current savings, projected expenses, and future financial needs to create a customized retirement plan. These systems provide simulations for different scenarios, allowing users to see how adjustments in spending, saving, or investments can impact their long-term financial security.

AI platforms may integrate with pension accounts, Social Security benefits, and annuities, offering real-time insights on optimizing withdrawals and maximizing benefits. By automating financial forecasting, older adults can make informed decisions that ensure they have sufficient funds to sustain their lifestyle throughout retirement.

Chapter 5: Expense Categorization

Managing expenses becomes effortless with AI-powered categorization tools. These applications automatically sort transactions into categories such as groceries, healthcare, and entertainment, providing older adults with a clear picture of where their money is going.

Expense categorization helps identify spending patterns and pinpoint areas where cost-cutting is possible. AI tools can also provide alerts when spending exceeds pre-set limits, allowing older adults to stay within budget and avoid unnecessary financial strain.

Chapter 6: Financial Literacy Tools

AI-driven financial literacy platforms offer interactive tutorials on a range of topics, including taxes, investments, and credit management. These tools simplify complex financial concepts, ensuring older adults can make informed decisions without being overwhelmed by technical jargon.

AI chatbots and virtual assistants provide on-demand guidance, answering questions in real-time and recommending educational resources tailored to older adult learning styles. By improving financial literacy, AI empowers older adults to take greater control over their financial well-being.

Chapter 7: Tax Preparation

AI-driven tax preparation tools streamline the filing process by identifying potential deductions, optimizing tax credits, and ensuring accuracy. These systems analyze financial documents, cross-check entries for errors, and provide step-by-step guidance for tax compliance.

AI platforms may even integrate with tax authorities to facilitate direct filing, reducing the time and effort required for manual submissions. By automating tax preparation, older adults can avoid costly mistakes and maximize their returns with minimal stress.

Chapter 8: Bill Payment Automation

Managing recurring bills can be challenging, but AI-powered automation tools simplify this process by tracking due dates and processing payments automatically. These systems send reminders for upcoming bills and notify users of insufficient funds, helping older adults avoid late fees and financial penalties.

By eliminating manual payment tasks, older adults can focus on other aspects of financial management while maintaining a strong credit history.

Chapter 9: Debt Management

AI tools can analyze an older adult's debt profile and develop customized repayment plans based on their financial situation. These platforms identify opportunities for consolidating loans, suggest priority repayment strategies, and provide insights into minimizing interest payments.

By automating debt tracking and providing real-time financial advice, AI empowers older adults to regain control over their finances and work toward financial independence.

Chapter 10: Legacy Planning

Estate planning is a critical aspect of financial management, and AI tools simplify this process by organizing wills, trusts, and beneficiary details. These systems provide checklists and legal guidance to ensure older adults' estate plans align with their wishes.

AI-powered platforms may also assist with tax-efficient estate planning, minimizing liabilities for beneficiaries. By leveraging AI for legacy planning, older adults can ensure their wealth is distributed according to their intentions while reducing stress for their loved ones.

Generative AI has transformed **financial management** by providing older adults with accessible, intelligent tools for budgeting, investment, fraud detection, and more. By integrating AI into daily financial planning, older adults can navigate their financial future with confidence, security, and peace of mind.

Chapter 1: Budgeting Assistance

AI-powered budgeting tools streamline financial planning by automatically categorizing income and expenses. These tools use machine learning algorithms to analyze spending patterns, helping older adults track their finances effortlessly. With visual dashboards, older adults can gain clear insights into their financial health, ensuring they remain within budget.

Over time, AI systems adapt to user behavior, offering personalized recommendations on cost-saving measures. For instance, they can alert users to recurring subscriptions they no longer use or suggest lower-cost alternatives for common expenses. AI tools may even allow users to set financial goals, while providing step-by-step guidance on how to achieve them.

By integrating AI into budgeting, older adults can eliminate the stress of manual expense tracking, focus on optimizing their resources, and maintain financial stability in retirement.

This chapter provides a collection of **clear and insightful scenarios** designed to enhance your ability to interact effectively with ChatGPT regarding **Budgeting Assistance**.

Each **scenario** is followed by:

- A carefully crafted **initial question** that prompts ChatGPT to analyze and respond thoughtfully to your scenario.
- A series of **follow-on questions** that demonstrate how to:

- Refine your original inquiry for better results.
- Seek clarification on ambiguous or complex responses.
- Request additional details to deepen your understanding.

By following this approach, you will learn strategies to improve the **relevance and accuracy** of ChatGPT's responses, ensuring more **productive and meaningful conversations**.

Let's Get Started: How to Use This Chapter

1. **Find a Topic of Interest**
   - Scroll through the chapter and pick a "block" that interests you.
   - Each block includes a **title, scenario, initial question, and follow-on questions**.
   - You can start with any block—there's no required order.

2. **Start-up ChatGPT and Ask the AI a Question**
   - Copy-and-paste the **Initial Question** into ChatGPT's chat box or type your own question.
   - The **Initial Question** helps focus ChatGPT's response.

3. **Review of the AI's Response**
   - Read and analyze ChatGPT's answer.
   - Decide if you need more information.

4. **Ask the AI Follow-Up Questions**
   - Use some or all of the **Follow-On Questions** provided or ask your own questions.

- More questions lead to deeper learning and better AI responses.

5. **Continue or Exit**
   - Keep exploring and refining your ChatGPT chat box inputs to improve the AI's response focus.
   - At any time, you can switch to another "block" of inquiry.
   - When you're done, simply exit the chat.

6. **The Goal of this Chapter and the Book**
   - Engage with ChatGPT as you would with a smart assistant to learn and improve how you use AI effectively!

AI-Powered Retirement Budget Planning

Scenario: A retiree wants to create a monthly budget to ensure their savings last.

Initial Question: "How can AI help me set up a monthly budget that aligns with my retirement savings?"

Follow-on Questions:

1. What factors should I consider when setting a sustainable retirement budget?
2. Can AI analyze my past expenses to recommend an optimal spending plan?
3. How do AI budgeting tools adapt to unexpected costs or emergencies?
4. What strategies are suggested by AI to reduce unnecessary spending?

5. Are there AI-powered alerts that notify me if I exceed my budget?
6. How can AI help me track my spending habits and adjust my budget accordingly?

Reducing Non-Essential Spending with AI

Scenario: An older adult is concerned about overspending on non-essential purchases.

Initial Question: "Can AI help me distinguish between essential and non-essential expenses?"

Follow-on Questions:

1. What methods does AI use to categorize my spending habits?
2. How can AI identify trends in my non-essential spending?
3. Are there AI tools that set spending limits for discretionary purchases?
4. Can AI provide weekly or monthly reports on my spending patterns?
5. How can I use AI to receive alerts before making impulse purchases?
6. What AI-driven strategies can help me cut down on non-essential expenses?

Optimizing Recurring Expenses with AI

Scenario: A retiree wants to find ways to save money on recurring bills.

Initial Question: "How can AI help me identify and reduce recurring expenses?"

Follow-on Questions:

1. Can AI detect subscriptions or memberships I'm no longer using?
2. How does AI compare utility or service providers to suggest cost-saving alternatives?
3. Are there AI tools that negotiate bills on my behalf?
4. How can AI track seasonal fluctuations in my utility bills and suggest ways to lower costs?
5. What budgeting apps can automatically cancel unused subscriptions?
6. Can AI analyze my spending patterns to recommend more affordable alternatives for recurring services?

Managing Medical Expenses with AI Budgeting Tools

Scenario: An older adult wants to track their medical expenses more effectively.

Initial Question: "What AI tools can help me monitor and budget for my medical expenses?"

Follow-on Questions:

1. How can AI categorize and track my healthcare costs over time?
2. Are there AI budgeting apps designed specifically for managing medical expenses?
3. Can AI analyze my insurance coverage and suggest ways to reduce out-of-pocket costs?

4. How does AI predict future medical expenses based on my past spending?
5. Can AI suggest affordable medication alternatives or discount programs?
6. How can AI help me set up a savings plan for medical emergencies?

AI-Assisted Fraud Prevention for Older Adults

Scenario: A retiree is worried about potential financial fraud or scams.

Initial Question: "How can AI help me detect and avoid financial scams?"

Follow-on Questions:

1. Are there AI-powered tools that monitor my accounts for suspicious activity?
2. How does AI analyze spending behavior to identify fraudulent transactions?
3. What alerts can AI provide if it detects potential scams in emails or messages?
4. Can AI recommend safe online shopping practices to prevent fraud?
5. How do AI-based budgeting tools protect my personal financial data?
6. What steps should I take if AI flags a potentially fraudulent transaction?

AI Budgeting for Large Purchases

Scenario: An older adult wants to plan for large purchases without affecting their budget.

Initial Question: "How can AI help me plan and save for big purchases?"

Follow-on Questions:

1. What budgeting strategies are suggested by AI for large purchases?
2. Can AI calculate the amount of money I need to save monthly for a major expense?
3. How does AI analyze past spending to ensure I can afford a big purchase?
4. Are there AI apps that create a step-by-step savings plan for a specific purchase?
5. Can AI track sales trends and suggest the best time to buy expensive items?
6. How do AI-driven alerts help me stay on track with my savings goal?

Ensuring Retirement Savings Last with AI

Scenario: An older adult wants to ensure they don't run out of money in retirement.

Initial Question: "How can AI assist me in making my retirement savings last?"

Follow-on Questions:

1. Can AI project my future expenses and suggest sustainable withdrawal rates?
2. How does AI factor in inflation when helping with long-term financial planning?
3. Are there AI tools that recommend investment strategies for retirees?
4. How can AI predict changes in my spending patterns over time?
5. What role can AI play in helping me adjust my budget for unexpected costs?
6. Can AI suggest part-time income opportunities that align with my skills?

Comparing Financial Strategies with AI

Scenario: A retiree wants to compare different financial planning strategies.

Initial Question: "What AI-driven budgeting tools can help me compare financial strategies?"

Follow-on Questions:

1. How do AI tools analyze the pros and cons of different budgeting strategies?
2. Can AI provide personalized financial recommendations based on my current situation?
3. What AI-powered financial calculators help me assess long-term outcomes?
4. How does AI adapt to changes in my income or expenses?

5. Can AI simulate different budgeting scenarios to help me choose the best plan?
6. What AI features allow for real-time adjustments to my financial plan?

Planning Inflation Adjustments with AI Budgeting Tools

Scenario: An older adult is worried about the impact of inflation on their budget.

Initial Question: "How can AI help me adjust my budget to account for inflation?"

Follow-on Questions:

1. Can AI predict how inflation will affect my cost of living over time?
2. How does AI track price trends for essential goods and services?
3. Are there AI tools that suggest cost-cutting measures to offset rising prices?
4. Can AI analyze my financial history and suggest adjustments for future stability?
5. What AI-powered budgeting techniques help me maintain my lifestyle despite inflation?
6. How does AI help retirees navigate changing economic conditions?

Finding the Best AI Budgeting Tool for Older Adults

Scenario: A retiree wants to find the best AI-driven budgeting app for their needs.

Initial Question: "What are the best AI budgeting tools for older adults?"

Follow-on Questions:

1. How do AI budgeting tools differ from traditional financial planners?
2. What features should I look for in an AI-powered budgeting app?
3. Are there AI budgeting tools designed specifically for retirees?
4. Can AI apps integrate with my bank accounts to track expenses automatically?
5. How does AI ensure my financial data remains secure?
6. What free or low-cost AI budgeting tools are available for older adults?

AI-Guided Debt Management for Retirees

Scenario: An older adult wants to manage existing debts while staying within their retirement budget.

Initial Question: "How can AI help me manage and pay off my debt more efficiently?"

Follow-on Questions:

1. Can AI analyze my debts and suggest the best repayment strategy?
2. How does AI prioritize which debts to pay off first?
3. Are there AI budgeting tools that automate debt tracking and payment reminders?
4. Can AI negotiate better interest rates or refinancing options for me?
5. How do AI tools compare different debt consolidation plans?
6. What strategies are recommended by AI to prevent new debt while maintaining financial stability?

AI-Driven Grocery Budgeting and Smart Shopping

Scenario: An older adult wants to reduce grocery expenses while maintaining a healthy diet.

Initial Question: "How can AI help me save money on groceries without compromising nutrition?"

Follow-on Questions:

1. Can AI track my grocery spending and suggest cost-effective alternatives?
2. Are there AI tools that compare prices across different grocery stores?
3. How can AI suggest meal plans that align with my budget and dietary needs?
4. Can AI alert me to discounts, coupons, or cash-back opportunities?
5. How does AI optimize grocery shopping lists to minimize waste?

6. What AI-powered grocery apps help older adults with budgeting and shopping efficiency?

AI Assistance in Managing Utility Costs

Scenario: A retiree is looking for ways to reduce electricity, water, and heating costs.

Initial Question: "How can AI help me lower my monthly utility bills?"

Follow-on Questions:

1. Can AI analyze my energy consumption and suggest cost-saving strategies?
2. How does AI compare different energy providers to find the best rates?
3. Are there AI tools that provide real-time usage tracking and alerts?
4. Can AI suggest home automation solutions to optimize energy efficiency?
5. What AI-driven habits can help reduce water and heating costs?
6. How do AI budgeting apps predict seasonal fluctuations in utility expenses?

AI-Based Travel Budgeting for Older Adults

Scenario: A retiree wants to take a vacation but needs to plan within a fixed budget.

Initial Question: "How can AI help me budget for an affordable vacation?"

Follow-on Questions:

1. Can AI compare travel deals and suggest the most cost-effective options?
2. How does AI calculate a daily spending plan for my trip?
3. Are there AI apps that track expenses in real time while traveling?
4. Can AI recommend budget-friendly strategies for accommodation and transportation?
5. How does AI help me find discounts on attractions and dining?
6. What AI-powered tools assist with foreign currency conversion and expense tracking?

AI-Powered Tax Planning for Retirees

Scenario: An older adult wants to ensure they maximize deductions and minimize tax liability.

Initial Question: "How can AI help me manage my taxes more efficiently in retirement?"

Follow-on Questions:

1. Can AI identify tax deductions or credits I might be eligible for?
2. How do AI tax tools help optimize withdrawals from retirement accounts?
3. Are there AI platforms that automate tax calculations for older adults?

4. Can AI provide personalized tax-saving strategies based on my financial situation?
5. How does AI detect potential errors or inconsistencies in my tax filings?
6. What AI-powered resources help with tax planning for retirees on fixed incomes?

AI Assistance in Charitable Giving and Philanthropy

Scenario: An older adult wants to donate to charities while ensuring it fits within their budget.

Initial Question: "How can AI help me budget charitable donations while maintaining financial security?"

Follow-on Questions:

1. Can AI analyze my finances to suggest an affordable giving plan?
2. Are there AI tools that recommend reputable charities based on my interests?
3. How does AI track my donations for tax deduction purposes?
4. Can AI compare the impact of one-time donations vs. recurring contributions?
5. What AI platforms help automate and optimize philanthropic giving?
6. How does AI ensure my donations are going to legitimate, high-impact organizations?

AI-Assisted Emergency Fund Planning

Scenario: A retiree wants to ensure they have a financial cushion for unexpected expenses.

Initial Question: "How can AI help me build and manage an emergency savings fund?"

Follow-on Questions:

1. What percentage of my income should I set aside for emergencies?
2. Can AI predict potential future financial risks based on my expenses?
3. How does AI track my savings progress and suggest adjustments?
4. Are there AI tools that automate contributions to an emergency fund?
5. What strategies are recommended by AI to balance emergency savings with daily expenses?
6. How do AI budgeting apps help manage unexpected costs without derailing financial plans?

AI Guidance on Affordable Home Maintenance

Scenario: An older adult homeowner wants to budget for home repairs and maintenance.

Initial Question: "How can AI help me manage home maintenance costs?"

Follow-on Questions:

1. Can AI predict upcoming home repairs based on past expenses?
2. Are there AI tools that compare contractor pricing and reviews?
3. How does AI track seasonal maintenance tasks to prevent costly repairs?
4. Can AI suggest DIY solutions for minor home fixes?
5. What AI budgeting apps help set aside funds for home-related expenses?
6. How does AI notify me of rebates or discounts on home improvement services?

AI-Powered Meal Planning for Cost Efficiency

Scenario: A retiree wants to maintain a nutritious diet while controlling food costs.

Initial Question: "How can AI help me plan budget-friendly, healthy meals?"

Follow-on Questions:

1. Can AI generate meal plans based on my dietary needs and budget?
2. How does AI compare grocery store prices to find the best deals?
3. Are there AI tools that track food waste and suggest efficient meal prep?
4. Can AI integrate with my grocery list to ensure I stay within budget?

5. What AI-powered apps help older adults optimize meal costs without sacrificing nutrition?
6. How does AI track seasonal produce prices to recommend cost-effective meal options?

AI-Assisted Subscription and Membership Management

Scenario: A retiree wants to ensure they are not overpaying for unused subscriptions.

Initial Question: "How can AI help me track and manage my subscriptions?"

Follow-on Questions:

1. Can AI identify subscriptions I no longer use and suggest cancellations?
2. How does AI compare pricing for different subscription services?
3. Are there AI tools that track free trials and notify me before auto-renewals?
4. Can AI negotiate better rates or discounts on my existing memberships?
5. What AI-driven strategies help older adults manage entertainment, fitness, and news subscriptions?
6. How does AI assist in consolidating multiple services to reduce costs?

Chapter 2: Fraud Detection

Financial fraud is a growing concern, particularly for older adults who may be more vulnerable to scams. AI-driven fraud detection tools provide an extra layer of security by monitoring financial transactions in real-time. These systems analyze patterns and flag suspicious activities, such as unauthorized transactions or phishing attempts.

Advanced fraud detection algorithms can detect inconsistencies in spending behavior and immediately notify users of potential threats. AI tools may integrate biometric authentication for enhanced security, reducing the risk of identity theft. Additionally, virtual assistants can educate older adults on common financial scams and provide real-time guidance when suspicious activities arise.

By leveraging AI for fraud detection, older adults can safeguard their finances, minimize risks, and enjoy peace of mind knowing their accounts are protected.

This chapter provides a collection of **clear and insightful scenarios** designed to enhance your ability to interact effectively with ChatGPT regarding **Fraud Detection**.

Each **scenario** is followed by:

- A carefully crafted **initial question** that prompts ChatGPT to analyze and respond thoughtfully to your scenario.
- A series of **follow-on questions** that demonstrate how to:

- Refine your original inquiry for better results.
- Seek clarification on ambiguous or complex responses.
- Request additional details to deepen your understanding.

By following this approach, you will learn strategies to improve the **relevance and accuracy** of ChatGPT's responses, ensuring more **productive and meaningful conversations**.

Let's Get Started: How to Use This Chapter

1. **Find a Topic of Interest**
   - Scroll through the chapter and pick a "block" that interests you.
   - Each block includes a **title, scenario, initial question, and follow-on questions**.
   - You can start with any block—there's no required order.

2. **Start-up ChatGPT and Ask the AI a Question**
   - Copy-and-paste the **Initial Question** into ChatGPT's chat box or type your own question.
   - The **Initial Question** helps focus ChatGPT's response.

3. **Review of the AI's Response**
   - Read and analyze ChatGPT's answer.
   - Decide if you need more information.

4. **Ask the AI Follow-Up Questions**
   - Use some or all of the **Follow-On Questions** provided or ask your own questions.

- More questions lead to deeper learning and better AI responses.

5. **Continue or Exit**
   - Keep exploring and refining your ChatGPT chat box inputs to improve the AI's response focus.
   - At any time, you can switch to another "block" of inquiry.
   - When you're done, simply exit the chat.

6. **The Goal of this Chapter and the Book**
   - Engage with ChatGPT as you would with a smart assistant to learn and improve how you use AI effectively!

AI Monitoring for Unauthorized Transactions

Scenario: An older adult notices unfamiliar charges on their credit card and wants to understand how AI can help detect and prevent such incidents.

Initial Question: "How can AI detect and alert me about unauthorized transactions?"

Follow-on Questions:

1. What types of spending patterns does AI analyze to identify fraud?
2. How does AI differentiate between a legitimate purchase and a fraudulent charge?
3. Can AI automatically freeze my account if it detects suspicious activity?

4. Are there AI-powered tools that provide real-time alerts for unusual spending?
5. How can AI help me dispute fraudulent transactions quickly?
6. What steps should I take if AI flags a suspicious transaction?

AI-Powered Phishing Detection

Scenario: A retiree receives an email claiming to be from their bank but suspects it might be fraudulent.

Initial Question: "How can AI help me identify and avoid phishing scams?"

Follow-on Questions:

1. What AI tools can scan emails and detect phishing attempts?
2. How does AI analyze website URLs to determine if they are legitimate or fraudulent?
3. Can AI alert me if I am about to enter sensitive information on a suspicious website?
4. What common characteristics do phishing emails share?
5. How does AI-powered email filtering help prevent scam messages from reaching my inbox?
6. What immediate actions should I take if I suspect I've interacted with a phishing attempt?

AI Fraud Alerts for Unusual Account Access

Scenario: An older adult receives a notification that someone tried to log into their bank account from another country.

Initial Question: "How can AI detect and prevent unauthorized access to my financial accounts?"

Follow-on Questions:

1. What AI security measures protect my accounts from unauthorized logins?
2. How does AI determine if a login attempt is legitimate or fraudulent?
3. Can AI recognize my typical login locations and flag unusual activity?
4. What AI-powered authentication methods enhance account security?
5. How does AI integrate with multi-factor authentication (MFA) for better protection?
6. What should I do if AI alerts me to an unauthorized login attempt?

AI Assistance in Detecting Identity Theft

Scenario: A retiree is concerned about their personal information being used for fraudulent activities.

Initial Question: "How can AI help me monitor and prevent identity theft?"

Follow-on Questions:

1. Can AI track my Social Security number for signs of misuse?
2. How does AI detect if my personal information has been sold on the dark web?
3. Are there AI tools that provide real-time alerts for changes to my credit report?

4. How can AI predict and prevent identity theft before it happens?
5. What AI-driven security measures can I implement to protect my identity?
6. How does AI help with recovering from identity theft if it occurs?

AI-Powered Scam Call Detection

Scenario: An older adult frequently receives suspicious phone calls asking for financial information.

Initial Question: "How can AI help me identify and block scam phone calls?"

Follow-on Questions:

1. What AI-powered apps can detect and block robocalls and phone scams?
2. How does AI recognize fraudulent speech patterns in scam calls?
3. Can AI provide real-time warnings if a call seems suspicious?
4. What AI tools transcribe and analyze calls to flag potential fraud?
5. How does AI compare phone numbers to known scam databases?
6. What precautions should I take if I receive a suspicious call?

AI Fraud Detection in Online Shopping

Scenario: An older adult wants to ensure they are shopping safely online and avoiding fraudulent sellers.

Initial Question: "How can AI help me detect scams when shopping online?"

Follow-on Questions:

1. What AI tools analyze website credibility before I make a purchase?
2. How does AI recognize counterfeit products or fraudulent sellers?
3. Can AI detect fake reviews and misleading product descriptions?
4. How does AI compare product pricing to prevent overpayment scams?
5. What AI-powered browser extensions enhance online shopping security?
6. How does AI alert me if I am about to enter payment details on an insecure website?

AI Protection Against Charity Scams

Scenario: A retiree wants to donate to a charity but is unsure if the organization is legitimate.

Initial Question: "How can AI help me verify the legitimacy of a charity before donating?"

Follow-on Questions:

1. What AI tools analyze nonprofit organizations for legitimacy?
2. Can AI detect fraudulent donation requests and fake charities?
3. How does AI track where my donation is being used?
4. Are there AI-powered databases that list reputable charities?
5. How can AI compare different charitable organizations based on transparency and impact?
6. What AI security measures ensure that my online donation is safe?

AI Assistance in Detecting Fake Investment Opportunities

Scenario: A retiree is offered an investment opportunity that seems too good to be true.

Initial Question: "How can AI help me verify whether an investment opportunity is a scam?"

Follow-on Questions:

1. What AI tools analyze investment opportunities for signs of fraud?
2. How does AI compare returns on investments to detect unrealistic promises?
3. Can AI track Ponzi schemes and other financial fraud tactics?
4. What AI-driven indicators suggest an investment might be a scam?
5. How does AI differentiate between legitimate investments and high-risk scams?
6. What steps should I take if AI warns me about a suspicious investment?

AI-Powered Password Security Monitoring

Scenario: An older adult wants to improve their online security to prevent unauthorized access.

Initial Question: "How can AI help me strengthen my passwords and protect my accounts?"

Follow-on Questions:

1. What AI tools generate and manage strong passwords for different accounts?
2. Can AI detect if my passwords have been leaked in a data breach?
3. How does AI integrate with password managers to enhance security?
4. What AI-powered authentication methods reduce the risk of password theft?
5. How often should AI recommend changing my passwords for security reasons?
6. How does AI evaluate the strength of my existing passwords?

AI Assistance in Detecting Fake Tech Support Scams

Scenario: An older adult receives a phone call claiming to be from a tech support company asking for access to their computer.

Initial Question: "How can AI help me recognize and avoid tech support scams?"

Follow-on Questions:

1. What AI tools detect and block fraudulent tech support calls?

2. How does AI analyze scam scripts and speech patterns?
3. Can AI provide real-time alerts if a tech support request seems suspicious?
4. What steps should I take if I have already engaged with a scammer?
5. How does AI differentiate between legitimate tech support and fraud attempts?
6. What AI-powered security features protect my computer from remote-access scams?

AI-Powered Credit Card Fraud Alerts

Scenario: An older adult wants to ensure that their credit card transactions are secure from fraud.

Initial Question: "How can AI detect and prevent credit card fraud in real time?"

Follow-on Questions:

1. What AI-driven systems analyze my spending behavior for fraud detection?
2. Can AI block or flag suspicious credit card transactions automatically?
3. How does AI determine whether a transaction is fraudulent or legitimate?
4. Are there AI tools that monitor credit card charges for unauthorized purchases?
5. What AI-based alerts can notify me instantly about suspicious activity?
6. How does AI help me dispute fraudulent charges on my credit card?

AI Protection Against Romance Scams

Scenario: An older adult engages in online dating but wants to avoid potential scams.

Initial Question: "How can AI help me identify and avoid online romance scams?"

Follow-on Questions:

1. What AI tools analyze online dating profiles for signs of fraud?
2. How does AI detect suspicious messaging patterns used by scammers?
3. Can AI identify stolen images used in fake profiles?
4. What AI-driven alerts notify me of red flags in online conversations?
5. How can AI compare my conversations to known scam tactics?
6. What should I do if AI detects signs of a romance scam in my interactions?

AI Monitoring for ATM and Debit Card Fraud

Scenario: An older adult frequently uses an ATM and wants to ensure secure transactions.

Initial Question: "How can AI help protect my debit card transactions from fraud?"

Follow-on Questions:

1. What AI tools track and analyze ATM withdrawals for unusual activity?
2. How does AI detect skimming devices or fraudulent ATM machines?
3. Can AI predict and warn me of high-risk ATM locations?
4. What AI-driven measures can secure my debit card transactions?
5. How does AI alert me to multiple withdrawals that could indicate fraud?
6. What AI-based solutions exist for recovering stolen funds from fraudulent withdrawals?

AI Assistance in Detecting Fake Job Offers

Scenario: A retiree is offered a remote job opportunity but suspects it may be a scam.

Initial Question: "How can AI help me determine if a job offer is legitimate?"

Follow-on Questions:

1. What AI tools analyze job postings for scam indicators?
2. Can AI compare a company's credentials against reputable business databases?
3. How does AI detect fraudulent payment requests in fake job offers?
4. Are there AI tools that check job recruiter credibility?
5. How does AI detect and flag job scams that request personal or financial information?

6. What steps should I take if AI determines a job offer is fraudulent?

AI-Powered Social Media Scam Detection

Scenario: An older adult wants to ensure they are not falling for scams on social media.

Initial Question: "How can AI help me recognize and avoid social media scams?"

Follow-on Questions:

1. What AI tools scan social media messages for scam tactics?
2. How does AI detect fake profiles used for scams?
3. Can AI identify fraudulent giveaways and contests?
4. How does AI track and block suspicious links sent via direct messages?
5. What AI-driven security features help prevent social media account hacking?
6. How should I respond if AI warns me about a potential scam on social media?

AI Assistance in Verifying Online Retailers

Scenario: A retiree wants to buy from a new online store but is unsure if it's legitimate.

Initial Question: "How can AI help me verify if an online retailer is trustworthy?"

Follow-on Questions:

1. What AI tools analyze online store legitimacy?
2. How does AI detect fraudulent e-commerce websites?
3. Can AI compare customer reviews to identify fake or paid feedback?
4. What AI-driven methods detect counterfeit or overpriced products?
5. How does AI determine if an online store follows proper security protocols?
6. What should I do if AI warns me about a high-risk retailer?

AI Protection Against Email Spoofing and Impersonation

Scenario: An older adult receives an email appearing to be from their bank but is unsure if it's real.

Initial Question: "How can AI detect and prevent email spoofing or impersonation scams?"

Follow-on Questions:

1. What AI tools analyze sender authenticity in emails?
2. How does AI detect email headers that indicate phishing attempts?
3. Can AI recognize language patterns used in impersonation scams?
4. What AI-driven security measures block spoofed emails?
5. How does AI differentiate between real company emails and fraudulent ones?
6. What steps should I take if AI confirms an email is fake?

AI Fraud Prevention in Peer-to-Peer Payment Apps

Scenario: An older adult uses peer-to-peer payment apps like PayPal or Venmo and wants fraud protection.

Initial Question: "How can AI help me detect and prevent fraud when using payment apps?"

Follow-on Questions:

1. What AI-powered features protect me from fraudulent payment requests?
2. How does AI detect suspicious activity in my transaction history?
3. Can AI flag requests from unverified or suspicious users?
4. What AI-driven security measures prevent unauthorized transactions?
5. How does AI recognize and prevent payment scams, such as overpayment fraud?
6. What should I do if AI detects an unusual payment request?

AI-Assisted Fraud Prevention in Real Estate and Rental Scams

Scenario: A retiree is looking for rental property online but wants to ensure the listing is legitimate.

Initial Question: "How can AI help me identify fraudulent real estate listings?"

Follow-on Questions:

1. What AI tools verify the legitimacy of rental listings?
2. How does AI detect if a listing uses stolen property photos?

3. Can AI compare rental prices in an area to flag suspiciously low offers?
4. What AI-driven methods detect fake landlords or property managers?
5. How does AI analyze lease agreements for signs of fraud?
6. What steps should I take if AI determines a rental listing is fraudulent?

AI-Powered Document Fraud Detection

Scenario: An older adult is asked to sign a financial document but wants to ensure it's legitimate.

Initial Question: "How can AI help me verify the authenticity of a financial document?"

Follow-on Questions:

1. What AI tools analyze documents for signs of forgery or tampering?
2. How does AI compare contract terms to legal templates for legitimacy?
3. Can AI detect inconsistencies in signatures or official seals?
4. What AI-driven methods flag suspicious clauses in financial agreements?
5. How does AI determine if a document was altered after signing?
6. What steps should I take if AI warns me about a potentially fraudulent document?

Chapter 3: Investment Advice

Investing can be overwhelming, especially for older adults unfamiliar with financial markets. AI-powered investment platforms simplify this process by offering personalized recommendations based on financial goals, risk tolerance, and market conditions.

These tools analyze vast amounts of financial data to provide tailored investment strategies. They can suggest diversified portfolios, automate rebalancing, and even predict market trends using predictive analytics. AI-driven financial advisors, also known as robo-advisors, offer cost-effective investment management, eliminating the need for expensive human advisors.

With AI-driven investment tools, older adults can confidently grow their wealth while minimizing risks and maintaining control over their financial future.

This chapter provides a collection of **clear and insightful scenarios** designed to enhance your ability to interact effectively with ChatGPT regarding **Investment Advice**.

Each **scenario** is followed by:

- A carefully crafted **initial question** that prompts ChatGPT to analyze and respond thoughtfully to your scenario.
- A series of **follow-on questions** that demonstrate how to:
    - Refine your original inquiry for better results.
    - Seek clarification on ambiguous or complex responses.

- Request additional details to deepen your understanding.

By following this approach, you will learn strategies to improve the **relevance and accuracy** of ChatGPT's responses, ensuring more **productive and meaningful conversations**.

Let's Get Started: How to Use This Chapter

1. **Find a Topic of Interest**
   - Scroll through the chapter and pick a "block" that interests you.
   - Each block includes a **title, scenario, initial question, and follow-on questions**.
   - You can start with any block—there's no required order.

2. **Start-up ChatGPT and Ask the AI a Question**
   - Copy-and-paste the **Initial Question** into ChatGPT's chat box or type your own question.
   - The **Initial Question** helps focus ChatGPT's response.

3. **Review of the AI's Response**
   - Read and analyze ChatGPT's answer.
   - Decide if you need more information.

4. **Ask the AI Follow-Up Questions**
   - Use some or all of the **Follow-On Questions** provided or ask your own questions.
   - More questions lead to deeper learning and better AI responses.

5. **Continue or Exit**
   - Keep exploring and refining your ChatGPT chat box inputs to improve the AI's response focus.
   - At any time, you can switch to another "block" of inquiry.
   - When you're done, simply exit the chat.

6. **The Goal of this Chapter and the Book**
   - Engage with ChatGPT as you would with a smart assistant to learn and improve how you use AI effectively!

AI Investment Strategies for Retirees

Scenario: A retiree wants to invest conservatively while ensuring their savings continue to grow.

Initial Question: "How can AI help me create a low-risk investment strategy for retirement?"

Follow-on Questions:

1. What AI tools analyze my risk tolerance and suggest investment options?
2. Can AI recommend a diversified portfolio to minimize market volatility?
3. How does AI use historical data to predict safe investment opportunities?
4. Are there AI-driven investment platforms designed specifically for retirees?
5. How does AI rebalance my portfolio based on changing financial needs?

6. What AI features help protect investments from sudden market downturns?

AI-Powered Robo-Advisors for Wealth Management

Scenario: An older adult wants to use a robo-advisor but is unsure how it works.

Initial Question: "How do AI-driven robo-advisors manage investments?"

Follow-on Questions:

1. How does AI assess my financial goals and risk tolerance?
2. What are the advantages of AI-driven robo-advisors over traditional financial planners?
3. Can AI automatically adjust my portfolio based on market changes?
4. How does AI monitor investment performance and suggest improvements?
5. Are there robo-advisors that cater specifically to retirees?
6. How do AI-powered advisors ensure my investments align with long-term financial goals?

AI for Identifying Safe Investment Opportunities

Scenario: A retiree wants to avoid high-risk investments but still grow their wealth.

Initial Question: "How can AI help me find safe and stable investment options?"

Follow-on Questions:

1. What AI tools analyze investment risks and returns?
2. How does AI determine whether an investment is safe for long-term growth?
3. Can AI compare different investment options based on risk levels?
4. How does AI predict future market trends for safer investments?
5. What AI-driven strategies help balance growth and security in a portfolio?
6. How does AI protect against economic downturns when choosing investments?

AI-Assisted Portfolio Diversification

Scenario: An older adult wants to ensure their investment portfolio is well-diversified.

Initial Question: "How can AI help me build a diversified investment portfolio?"

Follow-on Questions:

1. How does AI assess my current investments and suggest diversification strategies?
2. Can AI recommend sector-based diversification to minimize risk?
3. How does AI determine the best asset allocation for my financial goals?
4. What AI-driven models predict which industries will perform well in the future?

5. Can AI rebalance my portfolio periodically to maintain diversification?
6. What AI tools help track performance across different asset classes?

AI and Predictive Analytics for Stock Market Trends

Scenario: A retiree wants to understand how AI predicts stock market trends.

Initial Question: "How does AI use predictive analytics to forecast stock market movements?"

Follow-on Questions:

1. What data sources are analyzed by AI to identify stock market trends?
2. Can AI predict market downturns and suggest safer investment moves?
3. How does AI compare past market patterns to predict future performance?
4. What AI tools help monitor market fluctuations in real time?
5. Can AI help me identify undervalued stocks with growth potential?
6. How does AI-powered trading software use trend analysis for better investment decisions?

AI for Passive Income Investments

Scenario: An older adult wants to invest in assets that generate passive income.

Initial Question: "How can AI help me find investment opportunities that provide steady passive income?"

Follow-on Questions:

1. What AI tools analyze dividend stocks and fixed-income investments?
2. Can AI recommend real estate investments with high rental yield potential?
3. How does AI track and optimize returns from passive income investments?
4. What AI-driven strategies help retirees balance risk and steady cash flow?
5. How does AI identify high-yield bonds and low-volatility dividend stocks?
6. Can AI predict which passive income investments will remain stable over time?

AI Assistance in Evaluating Mutual Funds and Exchange-Traded Funds (ETFs)

Scenario: A retiree wants to invest in mutual funds or ETFs but needs guidance.

Initial Question: "How can AI help me evaluate and select the best mutual funds and ETFs?"

Follow-on Questions:

1. How does AI compare fund performance and risk levels?
2. Can AI analyze expense ratios and other fees to optimize investment choices?

3. How does AI predict the long-term stability of a mutual fund or ETF?
4. What AI tools track fund holdings and diversification strategies?
5. How does AI help rebalance ETF and mutual fund investments over time?
6. Can AI recommend socially responsible ETFs and mutual funds?

AI Investment Tools for Socially Responsible Investing (SRI)

Scenario: A retiree wants to invest in ethical and socially responsible companies.

Initial Question: "How can AI help me find socially responsible investment opportunities?"

Follow-on Questions:

1. What AI platforms evaluate companies based on ethical and environmental factors?
2. How does AI compare ESG (Environmental, Social, Governance) ratings of investments?
3. Can AI track corporate social responsibility trends for investment purposes?
4. What AI tools filter out companies that do not align with my values?
5. How does AI analyze long-term sustainability performance in investments?
6. What are the financial benefits of investing in socially responsible companies?

AI and Tax-Efficient Investment Strategies

Scenario: A retiree wants to minimize taxes on investment gains.

Initial Question: "How can AI help me create a tax-efficient investment strategy?"

Follow-on Questions:

1. What AI-driven tools help manage capital gains and tax liabilities?
2. How does AI optimize tax-loss harvesting strategies?
3. Can AI analyze my portfolio and suggest tax-advantaged investment accounts?
4. What AI methods help reduce taxes on dividend and interest income?
5. How does AI forecast future tax implications of different investment choices?
6. What AI-powered tax planning strategies work best for retirees?

AI Investment Advice for Estate Planning

Scenario: A retiree wants to ensure their investment portfolio is structured for inheritance.

Initial Question: "How can AI assist in investment planning for wealth transfer?"

Follow-on Questions:

1. How does AI evaluate the best tax strategies for passing down investments?

2. Can AI analyze trust funds and other estate planning investment options?
3. What AI tools help manage beneficiary designations for investment accounts?
4. How does AI optimize my investment portfolio for generational wealth?
5. What AI-driven financial models predict long-term estate growth?
6. How does AI assist in integrating investments with estate planning legal documents?

AI-Powered Retirement Income Planning

Scenario: A retiree wants to structure their investments to provide a steady retirement income.

Initial Question: "How can AI help me create a stable income stream in retirement?"

Follow-on Questions:

1. What AI tools analyze my investment portfolio for steady income generation?
2. Can AI recommend an optimal withdrawal strategy for my retirement savings?
3. How does AI balance risk and reward in income-generating investments?
4. What AI-driven models predict future income stability based on my investment choices?
5. Can AI suggest a mix of dividend stocks, bonds, and annuities for consistent income?
6. How does AI factor in inflation when designing a retirement income plan?

AI-Driven Real Estate Investment Insights

Scenario: A retiree is considering investing in rental properties and wants to use AI for guidance.

Initial Question: "How can AI help me find profitable real estate investments?"

Follow-on Questions:

1. What AI tools analyze rental market trends and property appreciation rates?
2. Can AI predict the best locations for real estate investments?
3. How does AI compare rental yields across different properties?
4. What AI-driven risk analysis can help me avoid bad real estate deals?
5. How does AI estimate future property maintenance and ownership costs?
6. What AI-based platforms automate rental property management?

AI-Assisted Risk Analysis for Investments

Scenario: An older adult investor wants to understand and manage investment risks better.

Initial Question: "How can AI help me assess and mitigate investment risks?"

Follow-on Questions:

1. What AI-driven tools analyze market volatility for risk management?
2. How does AI predict potential losses in my portfolio?
3. Can AI recommend risk-adjusted investments based on my financial situation?
4. What AI-based strategies help balance high-risk and low-risk investments?
5. How does AI track and alert me to potential investment risks in real time?
6. Can AI create risk simulations to evaluate different financial scenarios?

AI for Short-Term vs. Long-Term Investment Planning

Scenario: A retiree wants to allocate funds between short-term and long-term investments.

Initial Question: "How can AI help me balance short-term and long-term investments?"

Follow-on Questions:

1. What AI tools compare the risks and returns of short-term vs. long-term investments?
2. How does AI assess my financial goals to recommend the best investment mix?
3. Can AI predict short-term market trends for better decision-making?
4. How does AI optimize liquidity while maintaining long-term growth?

5. What AI-based strategies ensure financial stability across different investment timeframes?
6. Can AI automatically rebalance my portfolio based on changing market conditions?

AI for Monitoring and Adjusting Investments

Scenario: An older adult wants AI to help track and adjust their investments over time.

Initial Question: "How can AI monitor my investments and suggest adjustments?"

Follow-on Questions:

1. What AI-driven platforms provide real-time portfolio tracking?
2. How does AI analyze market shifts and recommend investment reallocations?
3. Can AI automatically rebalance my portfolio to maintain diversification?
4. What AI tools send alerts when my investments reach a certain threshold?
5. How does AI factor in external economic events when adjusting portfolios?
6. Can AI predict when I should buy, hold, or sell specific assets?

AI-Powered Stock Market News Analysis

Scenario: A retiree wants to stay informed about stock market developments using AI.

Initial Question: "How can AI help me analyze financial news for investment decisions?"

Follow-on Questions:

1. What AI tools summarize and analyze market news for investors?
2. How does AI differentiate between market hype and meaningful trends?
3. Can AI track how news events impact my specific investments?
4. What AI-driven alerts notify me of major financial developments?
5. How does AI compare multiple news sources for unbiased investment insights?
6. Can AI predict market reactions to breaking financial news?

AI-Powered Investment Fee Optimization

Scenario: An older adult wants to reduce investment management costs without sacrificing returns.

Initial Question: "How can AI help me minimize fees while optimizing my investments?"

Follow-on Questions:

1. What AI tools analyze investment fees and suggest lower-cost alternatives?
2. Can AI compare the expense ratios of mutual funds and ETFs?
3. How does AI calculate the long-term impact of investment fees on returns?

4. What AI-based strategies help reduce unnecessary trading fees?
5. How does AI suggest cost-effective investment platforms?
6. Can AI automate portfolio management to minimize unnecessary costs?

AI Assistance in Retirement Savings Growth

Scenario: A retiree wants AI guidance on growing their retirement savings over time.

Initial Question: "How can AI help me maximize the growth of my retirement savings?"

Follow-on Questions:

1. What AI tools suggest high-performing but low-risk retirement investments?
2. Can AI recommend tax-efficient strategies for retirement accounts?
3. How does AI predict long-term portfolio growth?
4. What AI-driven models calculate the best withdrawal rates for retirement savings?
5. How does AI optimize contributions to retirement investment accounts?
6. Can AI automate adjustments to my savings strategy based on market conditions?

AI for International Investment Opportunities

Scenario: An older adult investor wants to explore global investment options.

Initial Question: "How can AI help me identify profitable international investments?"

Follow-on Questions:

1. What AI tools analyze global market trends for investment opportunities?
2. How does AI compare international stock markets for growth potential?
3. Can AI predict currency exchange rate risks for international investments?
4. What AI-based strategies help diversify investments across global markets?
5. How does AI evaluate foreign real estate investment opportunities?
6. What AI-driven platforms simplify cross-border investing for retirees?

AI-Powered Annuity and Fixed Income Investment Analysis

Scenario: A retiree wants to invest in annuities and fixed-income securities.

Initial Question: "How can AI help me evaluate annuities and fixed-income investments?"

Follow-on Questions:

1. What AI tools compare different types of annuities for retirees?
2. How does AI analyze the long-term benefits of fixed-income investments?
3. Can AI predict inflation-adjusted returns for annuities?
4. What AI-based strategies optimize bond investments for stability?
5. How does AI evaluate municipal bonds and other tax-free fixed-income options?
6. Can AI suggest a mix of annuities and bonds to ensure steady income?

Chapter 4: Retirement Planning

AI-based retirement planning tools evaluate an older adult's current savings, projected expenses, and future financial needs to create a customized retirement plan. These systems provide simulations for different scenarios, allowing users to see how adjustments in spending, saving, or investments can impact their long-term financial security.

AI platforms may integrate with pension accounts, Social Security benefits, and annuities, offering real-time insights on optimizing withdrawals and maximizing benefits. By automating financial forecasting, older adults can make informed decisions that ensure they have sufficient funds to sustain their lifestyle throughout retirement.

This chapter provides a collection of **clear and insightful scenarios** designed to enhance your ability to interact effectively with ChatGPT regarding **Retirement Planning**.

Each **scenario** is followed by:

- A carefully crafted **initial question** that prompts ChatGPT to analyze and respond thoughtfully to your scenario.
- A series of **follow-on questions** that demonstrate how to:
    - Refine your original inquiry for better results.
    - Seek clarification on ambiguous or complex responses.
    - Request additional details to deepen your understanding.

By following this approach, you will learn strategies to improve the **relevance and accuracy** of ChatGPT's responses, ensuring more **productive and meaningful conversations**.

Let's Get Started: How to Use This Chapter

1. **Find a Topic of Interest**
   - Scroll through the chapter and pick a "block" that interests you.
   - Each block includes a **title, scenario, initial question, and follow-on questions**.
   - You can start with any block—there's no required order.

2. **Start-up ChatGPT and Ask the AI a Question**
   - Copy-and-paste the **Initial Question** into ChatGPT's chat box or type your own question.
   - The **Initial Question** helps focus ChatGPT's response.

3. **Review of the AI's Response**
   - Read and analyze ChatGPT's answer.
   - Decide if you need more information.

4. **Ask the AI Follow-Up Questions**
   - Use some or all of the **Follow-On Questions** provided or ask your own questions.
   - More questions lead to deeper learning and better AI responses.

5. **Continue or Exit**

    - Keep exploring and refining your ChatGPT chat box inputs to improve the AI's response focus.
    - At any time, you can switch to another "block" of inquiry.
    - When you're done, simply exit the chat.

6. **The Goal of this Chapter and the Book**

    - Engage with ChatGPT as you would with a smart assistant to learn and improve how you use AI effectively!

AI-Based Retirement Savings Forecasting

Scenario: An older adult wants to ensure their retirement savings will last throughout their lifetime.

Initial Question: "How can AI help me forecast whether my retirement savings will be sufficient?"

Follow-on Questions:

1. What AI tools analyze my current savings and project future financial needs?
2. Can AI simulate different spending scenarios to determine how long my savings will last?
3. How does AI factor in inflation and healthcare costs in retirement forecasts?
4. Can AI suggest adjustments to my savings strategy to improve financial security?
5. What AI-driven recommendations can help me extend my retirement funds?

6. How does AI compare different withdrawal strategies for optimal savings longevity?

AI Assistance in Social Security Optimization

Scenario: A retiree wants to maximize their Social Security benefits.

Initial Question: "How can AI help me determine the best time to claim Social Security?"

Follow-on Questions:

1. What AI-driven tools analyze my work history and benefits eligibility?
2. Can AI compare different claiming strategies to maximize my lifetime benefits?
3. How does AI factor in life expectancy and spousal benefits when making recommendations?
4. What AI models predict the impact of delaying Social Security claims?
5. Can AI integrate Social Security with other retirement income sources for a complete plan?
6. How does AI estimate the long-term financial impact of my claiming decision?

AI for Retirement Expense Management

Scenario: An older adult wants to track and manage their expenses efficiently in retirement.

Initial Question: "How can AI help me monitor and control my retirement expenses?"

Follow-on Questions:

1. What AI tools categorize and track retirement spending?
2. Can AI detect areas where I may be overspending?
3. How does AI suggest budget adjustments to align with my financial goals?
4. Can AI predict future expense trends based on my current lifestyle?
5. What AI-driven alerts notify me if I exceed my planned spending limits?
6. How does AI optimize expense tracking for better financial decision-making?

AI-Powered Retirement Income Planning

Scenario: A retiree wants to structure their investments and withdrawals for a steady retirement income.

Initial Question: "How can AI help me create a reliable income plan in retirement?"

Follow-on Questions:

1. What AI tools analyze my retirement income sources and suggest an optimal withdrawal strategy?
2. Can AI recommend the best mix of investments to sustain my income?
3. How does AI adjust my withdrawal plan based on market fluctuations?
4. Can AI predict future changes in my income needs?

5. What AI-based strategies help maintain a steady income while minimizing tax liability?
6. How does AI integrate Social Security, pensions, and annuities into my retirement plan?

AI-Driven Investment Strategies for Retirees

Scenario: An older adult wants to invest wisely without taking on excessive risk.

Initial Question: "How can AI help me create a low-risk investment strategy for retirement?"

Follow-on Questions:

1. What AI tools analyze risk tolerance and suggest retirement-friendly investments?
2. Can AI recommend a diversified portfolio to minimize market volatility?
3. How does AI predict stable, long-term investment opportunities?
4. What AI-driven strategies protect against economic downturns?
5. How does AI compare fixed-income investments to maintain stability?
6. Can AI help me balance growth with security in my retirement portfolio?

AI for Healthcare Cost Planning in Retirement

Scenario: A retiree is concerned about rising healthcare costs affecting their financial stability.

Initial Question: "How can AI help me plan for healthcare expenses in retirement?"

Follow-on Questions:

1. What AI tools predict future healthcare costs based on my medical history?
2. How does AI integrate Medicare and other insurance plans into my financial planning?
3. Can AI compare different supplemental insurance policies for better coverage?
4. How does AI estimate the cost of long-term care services?
5. What AI-driven strategies help older adults prepare for unexpected medical expenses?
6. How does AI recommend savings adjustments for rising healthcare costs?

AI Assistance in Downsizing and Relocating for Retirement

Scenario: A retiree wants to downsize or relocate to manage costs better.

Initial Question: "How can AI help me decide if downsizing or relocating is the right financial move?"

Follow-on Questions:

1. What AI tools analyze housing costs in different retirement locations?
2. Can AI compare the cost of living between cities to determine the best option?
3. How does AI predict the financial impact of selling my home and moving?
4. What AI-driven real estate platforms suggest best areas for retirees?
5. How does AI calculate long-term savings from downsizing?
6. Can AI recommend ways to maximize profits when selling my current home?

AI-Powered Tax Planning for Retirees

Scenario: An older adult wants to minimize taxes on their retirement income.

Initial Question: "How can AI help me create a tax-efficient retirement plan?"

Follow-on Questions:

1. What AI tools analyze my tax obligations and suggest savings strategies?
2. Does AI recommend optimal withdrawal strategies to minimize taxes?
3. Can AI identify tax credits and deductions for retirees?
4. How does AI optimize tax-efficient investment accounts like Roth older adult retirement accounts (IRAs)?
5. What AI-based models estimate tax savings from charitable giving?

6. Can AI provide insights on the best states for tax-friendly retirement?

AI-Assisted Estate and Legacy Planning

Scenario: A retiree wants to ensure their assets are managed properly for heirs.

Initial Question: "How can AI help me with estate and legacy planning?"

Follow-on Questions:

1. What AI tools analyze my estate and suggest strategies for wealth transfer?
2. Can AI optimize my estate plan to minimize tax burdens for my heirs?
3. How does AI integrate with wills and trusts for asset protection?
4. What AI-driven recommendations help me plan for charitable giving?
5. How does AI monitor legal changes that may impact my estate plan?
6. Can AI assist in setting up a trust to secure my family's financial future?

AI-Driven Financial Simulations for Retirement Scenarios

Scenario: A retiree wants to see how different financial decisions impact their long-term security.

Initial Question: "How can AI simulate different retirement scenarios to help me plan better?"

Follow-on Questions:

1. What AI-driven simulation tools help me evaluate different retirement strategies?
2. How does AI compare various investment and withdrawal scenarios?
3. Can AI forecast how market changes will affect my long-term savings?
4. What AI-powered risk analysis helps prepare for economic downturns?
5. How does AI simulate different healthcare cost scenarios in retirement?
6. Can AI suggest modifications to my plan based on changing financial conditions?

AI for Early Retirement Planning

Scenario: A working professional wants to determine if early retirement is financially feasible.

Initial Question: "How can AI help me assess if I can retire early?"

Follow-on Questions:

1. What AI tools analyze my savings and expenses to determine early retirement feasibility?
2. Can AI project my future expenses based on different retirement ages?

3. How does AI calculate the impact of delaying Social Security benefits?
4. What AI-driven strategies can help me achieve early retirement faster?
5. Can AI recommend passive income sources to sustain early retirement?
6. How does AI account for inflation and healthcare costs in early retirement planning?

AI Assistance in Retirement Withdrawal Strategies

Scenario: A retiree wants to optimize their withdrawal strategy to avoid running out of money.

Initial Question: "How can AI help me create a sustainable withdrawal strategy in retirement?"

Follow-on Questions:

1. What AI tools analyze my portfolio to determine an optimal withdrawal rate?
2. How does AI compare the 4% rule with other withdrawal strategies?
3. Can AI simulate different economic conditions that evaluate withdrawal scenarios?
4. How does AI suggest tax-efficient withdrawals to minimize tax burdens?
5. Can AI recommend adjustments if market downturns impact my savings?
6. What AI-driven alerts notify me when it's time to adjust my withdrawal plan?

AI for Pension Planning and Optimization

Scenario: An older adult is unsure how to maximize their pension benefits.

Initial Question: "How can AI help me optimize my pension payouts?"

Follow-on Questions:

1. What AI tools analyze different pension payout options?
2. How does AI compare lump-sum payouts versus monthly pension payments?
3. Can AI predict the long-term financial impact of my pension choices?
4. What AI-driven models integrate pension planning with Social Security and investments?
5. How does AI factor in inflation adjustments when planning for pension benefits?
6. Can AI provide insights into pension fund stability and future payout risks?

AI-Powered Inflation Protection for Retirement Savings

Scenario: A retiree is concerned about inflation eroding their purchasing power.

Initial Question: "How can AI help me protect my retirement savings from inflation?"

Follow-on Questions:

1. What AI tools analyze the historical impact of inflation on retirement savings?
2. How does AI recommend investments that hedge against inflation?
3. Can AI simulate different inflation scenarios and their impact on my finances?
4. How does AI track inflation-adjusted income needs in retirement?
5. What AI-driven strategies help retirees maintain their lifestyle despite rising costs?
6. Can AI suggest cost-cutting measures to offset inflation effects?

AI for Healthcare and Long-Term Care Planning

Scenario: A retiree wants to plan for potential long-term care needs.

Initial Question: "How can AI help me prepare financially for long-term care expenses?"

Follow-on Questions:

1. What AI tools estimate future long-term care costs based on my health profile?
2. How does AI compare different long-term care insurance policies?
3. Can AI predict when I may need assisted living or home healthcare?
4. How does AI recommend savings strategies for long-term care?

5. What AI-driven alerts notify me of rising healthcare costs?
6. Can AI help me integrate Medicaid planning into my retirement strategy?

AI for Retirement Debt Reduction Planning

Scenario: A retiree wants to eliminate debt before or during retirement.

Initial Question: "How can AI help me develop a plan to pay off debt before retirement?"

Follow-on Questions:

1. What AI tools analyze my current debts and suggest a repayment plan?
2. How does AI compare the benefits of paying off debt versus investing?
3. Can AI simulate different debt payoff strategies and their long-term impact?
4. How does AI track my progress toward becoming debt-free in retirement?
5. What AI-driven alerts notify me when I reach critical debt reduction milestones?
6. Can AI suggest ways to reduce interest payments on existing debt?

AI-Assisted Budgeting for Fixed Income in Retirement

Scenario: A retiree wants to manage their finances while living on a fixed income.

Initial Question: "How can AI help me budget effectively with a fixed retirement income?"

Follow-on Questions:

1. What AI tools create a personalized retirement budget based on my income?
2. How does AI categorize expenses to prevent overspending?
3. Can AI track fluctuations in my fixed income sources and adjust accordingly?
4. How does AI predict future expenses to help with long-term budgeting?
5. What AI-driven alerts warn me if I'm exceeding my monthly budget?
6. Can AI suggest cost-cutting measures without sacrificing my quality of life?

AI for Financial Fraud Protection in Retirement

Scenario: A retiree wants to safeguard their assets from fraud and scams.

Initial Question: "How can AI help me detect and prevent financial fraud in retirement?"

Follow-on Questions:

1. What AI tools monitor my accounts for suspicious activity?
2. How does AI detect fraudulent transactions and alert me in real-time?
3. Can AI analyze my spending behavior to flag unusual purchases?

4. How does AI integrate with credit monitoring services to prevent identity theft?
5. What AI-driven strategies help retirees protect their personal and financial information?
6. How does AI educate older adults on common financial scams and fraud tactics?

AI Assistance in Charitable Giving and Legacy Planning

Scenario: A retiree wants to incorporate charitable giving into their retirement plan.

Initial Question: "How can AI help me plan for charitable donations while maintaining financial stability?"

Follow-on Questions:

1. What AI tools analyze my finances to suggest an affordable giving plan?
2. Can AI recommend reputable charities aligned with my values?
3. How does AI track my donations for tax deduction purposes?
4. What AI-driven insights help maximize the impact of my charitable giving?
5. Can AI compare the financial benefits of one-time donations versus recurring contributions?
6. How does AI integrate charitable giving into estate planning?

AI-Driven Retirement Relocation Planning

Scenario: A retiree is considering relocating to a different state or country for a better financial situation.

Initial Question: "How can AI help me decide the best location for my retirement?"

Follow-on Questions:

1. What AI tools compare cost-of-living data for different retirement destinations?
2. How does AI analyze tax implications of retiring in various states or countries?
3. Can AI predict future economic trends that may affect my chosen location?
4. How does AI factor in healthcare access and quality in different areas?
5. What AI-driven real estate tools suggest affordable housing options for retirees?
6. Can AI estimate how my retirement savings will last based on my preferred location?

Chapter 5: Expense Categorization

Managing expenses becomes effortless with AI-powered categorization tools. These applications automatically sort transactions into categories such as groceries, healthcare, and entertainment, providing older adults with a clear picture of where their money is going.

Expense categorization helps identify spending patterns and pinpoint areas where cost-cutting is possible. AI tools can also provide alerts when spending exceeds pre-set limits, allowing older adults to stay within budget and avoid unnecessary financial strain.

This chapter provides a collection of **clear and insightful scenarios** designed to enhance your ability to interact effectively with ChatGPT regarding **Expense Categorization**.

Each **scenario** is followed by:

- A carefully crafted **initial question** that prompts ChatGPT to analyze and respond thoughtfully to your scenario.
- A series of **follow-on questions** that demonstrate how to:
  - Refine your original inquiry for better results.
  - Seek clarification on ambiguous or complex responses.
  - Request additional details to deepen your understanding.

By following this approach, you will learn strategies to improve the **relevance and accuracy** of ChatGPT's responses, ensuring more **productive and meaningful conversations**.

Let's Get Started: How to Use This Chapter

1. **Find a Topic of Interest**
   - Scroll through the chapter and pick a "block" that interests you.
   - Each block includes a **title, scenario, initial question, and follow-on questions**.
   - You can start with any block—there's no required order.

2. **Start-up ChatGPT and Ask the AI a Question**
   - Copy-and-paste the **Initial Question** into ChatGPT's chat box or type your own question.
   - The **Initial Question** helps focus ChatGPT's response.

3. **Review of the AI's Response**
   - Read and analyze ChatGPT's answer.
   - Decide if you need more information.

4. **Ask the AI Follow-Up Questions**
   - Use some or all of the **Follow-On Questions** provided or ask your own questions.
   - More questions lead to deeper learning and better AI responses.

5. **Continue or Exit**
   - Keep exploring and refining your ChatGPT chat box inputs to improve the AI's response focus.
   - At any time, you can switch to another "block" of inquiry.
   - When you're done, simply exit the chat.

6. **The Goal of this Chapter and the Book**
    - Engage with ChatGPT as you would with a smart assistant to learn and improve how you use AI effectively!

AI for Automatic Expense Categorization

Scenario: A retiree wants to track their spending habits more effectively.

Initial Question: "How can AI help me automatically categorize my expenses?"

Follow-on Questions:

1. What AI tools analyze and categorize my transactions?
2. How does AI differentiate between essential and non-essential expenses?
3. Can AI create custom categories based on my unique spending habits?
4. How does AI track cash versus digital transactions?
5. What AI-powered alerts notify me of unusual spending in specific categories?
6. How can AI help me set and maintain budget limits for different expense categories?

AI for Grocery Spending Analysis

Scenario: An older adult wants to reduce their grocery expenses.

Initial Question: "How can AI help me analyze and manage my grocery spending?"

Follow-on Questions:

1. What AI tools categorize grocery purchases and track price trends?
2. Can AI suggest cheaper alternatives for frequently purchased grocery items?
3. How does AI compare spending at different stores to identify cost savings?
4. Can AI alert me when I exceed my monthly grocery budget?
5. What AI-driven recommendations help me buy in bulk or find discounts?
6. How does AI track perishable food waste and suggest smarter grocery shopping?

AI for Healthcare Expense Tracking

Scenario: A retiree wants to monitor and manage their medical expenses.

Initial Question: "How can AI help me track and categorize my healthcare costs?"

Follow-on Questions:

1. What AI tools categorize medical expenses, including prescriptions and doctor visits?
2. Can AI analyze trends in my healthcare spending and suggest cost-saving options?
3. How does AI help me compare medical service prices in my area?

4. Can AI provide reminders for medical bill payments and insurance claims?
5. What AI-driven insights predict future healthcare costs based on past expenses?
6. How does AI assist in finding discounts or financial assistance for medical bills?

AI for Utility Bill Management

Scenario: A retiree wants to monitor and reduce their electricity, water, and gas expenses.

Initial Question: "How can AI help me track and lower my utility bills?"

Follow-on Questions:

1. What AI tools categorize and monitor my monthly utility expenses?
2. How does AI detect seasonal spikes in electricity and heating costs?
3. Can AI compare my utility bills with similar households?
4. What AI-driven alerts notify me of potential energy waste?
5. Can AI suggest alternative energy providers or budget-friendly plans?
6. How does AI predict future utility costs based on historical trends?

AI for Subscription and Membership Tracking

Scenario: An older adult wants to keep track of their active subscriptions and cancel unused ones.

Initial Question: "How can AI help me manage my subscriptions and memberships?"

Follow-on Questions:

1. What AI tools categorize and track all my recurring subscriptions?
2. Can AI detect unused or duplicate subscriptions?
3. How does AI compare prices for subscription-based services?
4. Can AI notify me before free trials convert to paid subscriptions?
5. What AI-driven recommendations help reduce monthly subscription costs?
6. How does AI assist in automating subscription cancellations?

AI for Dining and Entertainment Budgeting

Scenario: A retiree wants to monitor their spending on dining out and entertainment.

Initial Question: "How can AI help me track and manage my dining and entertainment expenses?"

Follow-on Questions:

1. What AI tools categorize restaurant and entertainment spending?

2. Can AI analyze spending patterns and suggest cost-saving alternatives?
3. How does AI provide personalized budget recommendations for leisure activities?
4. Can AI suggest discounted entertainment options based on my interests?
5. What AI-driven insights help reduce spending on non-essential outings?
6. How does AI track group dining expenses and split costs fairly?

AI for Travel and Vacation Expense Categorization

Scenario: An older adult wants to budget effectively for upcoming trips.

Initial Question: "How can AI help me categorize and manage my travel expenses?"

Follow-on Questions:

1. What AI tools track and categorize travel-related costs?
2. How does AI compare travel expenses across different trips?
3. Can AI predict the total cost of an upcoming vacation?
4. What AI-driven alerts notify me of travel deals and cost-saving opportunities?
5. How does AI integrate travel expenses into my overall budget?
6. Can AI recommend destinations that fit within my budget?

AI for Home Maintenance and Repair Costs

Scenario: A retiree wants to track home maintenance expenses and plan for future repairs.

Initial Question: "How can AI help me manage and categorize my home maintenance costs?"

Follow-on Questions:

1. What AI tools track spending on home repairs and upgrades?
2. How does AI estimate future maintenance costs based on past spending?
3. Can AI categorize home expenses into urgent and non-urgent repairs?
4. What AI-driven recommendations help me find cost-effective home service providers?
5. Can AI notify me when it's time for routine maintenance?
6. How does AI compare contractor estimates for home improvement projects?

AI for Pet Care Expenses

Scenario: A retiree with pets wants to budget for pet-related costs.

Initial Question: "How can AI help me track and manage my pet care expenses?"

Follow-on Questions:

1. What AI tools categorize expenses related to pet food, vet visits, and grooming?

2. Can AI analyze my pet-related spending trends and suggest cost-saving tips?
3. How does AI compare pet insurance plans and veterinary costs?
4. Can AI notify me when it's time for routine vet checkups or vaccinations?
5. What AI-driven insights help track and budget for emergency pet care?
6. How does AI recommend affordable pet supplies based on my preferences?

AI for Charitable Giving and Donations

Scenario: An older adult wants to monitor and optimize their charitable donations.

Initial Question: "How can AI help me track and categorize my charitable contributions?"

Follow-on Questions:

1. What AI tools analyze and categorize my donations for tax purposes?
2. Can AI suggest reputable charities based on my interests and budget?
3. How does AI track recurring versus one-time donations?
4. What AI-driven insights help me maximize the impact of my charitable giving?
5. Can AI compare the financial benefits of direct giving versus donor-advised funds?
6. How does AI predict the amount of money I can safely allocate to charitable contributions?

AI for Categorizing Unexpected Expenses

Scenario: A retiree wants to track and plan for unforeseen expenses.

Initial Question: "How can AI help me categorize and prepare for unexpected expenses?"

Follow-on Questions:

1. What AI tools analyze my past spending to identify patterns in unexpected costs?
2. Can AI suggest an emergency fund based on my historical expenses?
3. How does AI differentiate between regular and one-time emergency expenses?
4. What AI-driven alerts notify me of unusual-spending spikes?
5. Can AI recommend ways to reduce the impact of unexpected costs on my budget?
6. How does AI integrate emergency expenses into my overall financial plan?

AI for Categorizing Transportation Expenses

Scenario: An older adult wants to monitor their transportation spending, including fuel, maintenance, and public transit.

Initial Question: "How can AI help me track and categorize my transportation expenses?"

Follow-on Questions:

1. What AI tools categorize my transportation costs into fuel, maintenance, and public transit?
2. Can AI compare my fuel spending across different months and seasons?
3. How does AI analyze the cost-effectiveness of owning a car versus using public transportation?
4. Can AI suggest cheaper gas stations or maintenance providers?
5. What AI-driven alerts notify me of upcoming car maintenance expenses?
6. How does AI factor in depreciation costs when calculating overall vehicle expenses?

AI for Managing Gift and Holiday Expenses

Scenario: A retiree wants to budget better for holiday shopping and gift-giving.

Initial Question: "How can AI help me track and manage my gift and holiday expenses?"

Follow-on Questions:

1. What AI tools categorize holiday spending separately from my regular budget?
2. Can AI analyze past holiday spending to predict my future budget needs?
3. How does AI provide alerts if I’m exceeding my planned holiday budget?
4. Can AI recommend ways to save on gifts and holiday travel?

5. What AI-driven strategies help me spread out holiday expenses throughout the year?
6. How does AI track discounts and seasonal sales for smarter holiday shopping?

AI for Entertainment Subscriptions and Streaming Services

Scenario: A retiree wants to manage multiple streaming and entertainment subscriptions.

Initial Question: "How can AI help me categorize and manage my entertainment subscriptions?"

Follow-on Questions:

1. What AI tools track and categorize my streaming and entertainment expenses?
2. Can AI analyze my usage patterns and suggest which subscriptions to cancel?
3. How does AI compare different streaming service prices for cost-effectiveness?
4. Can AI alert me before a subscription auto-renews?
5. What AI-driven insights help me bundle or switch to more affordable entertainment options?
6. How does AI predict future subscription price increases and recommend budget adjustments?

AI for Organizing Home Insurance and Property Tax Expenses

Scenario: An older adult homeowner wants to track home insurance and property tax payments.

Initial Question: "How can AI help me categorize and manage my home-related expenses?"

Follow-on Questions:

1. What AI tools categorize and track my property tax and home insurance payments?
2. Can AI compare home insurance policies and suggest cost-saving alternatives?
3. How does AI predict potential increases in property taxes and insurance premiums?
4. Can AI set reminders for property tax deadlines and insurance renewals?
5. What AI-driven insights help me optimize homeownership costs?
6. How does AI analyze my home's value and suggest refinancing options if needed?

AI for Dining and Grocery Balance Tracking

Scenario: A retiree wants to ensure they maintain a balanced budget between dining out and grocery shopping.

Initial Question: "How can AI help me track and balance my grocery and dining expenses?"

Follow-on Questions:

1. What AI tools categorize dining and grocery expenses separately?
2. Can AI analyze my spending habits and suggest cost-saving meal plans?

3. How does AI track restaurant promotions or grocery store discounts?
4. Can AI provide alerts if I exceed my dining-out budget?
5. What AI-driven insights help me decide whether to cook at home or eat out?
6. How does AI analyze my diet-related expenses and suggest healthier, budget-friendly alternatives?

AI for Education and Lifelong Learning Expenses

Scenario: A retiree wants to track their spending on courses, books, and learning materials.

Initial Question: "How can AI help me categorize and manage my education-related expenses?"

Follow-on Questions:

1. What AI tools categorize online courses, books, and educational subscriptions?
2. Can AI analyze my spending trends on educational materials over time?
3. How does AI compare costs for similar courses or certifications?
4. Can AI suggest free or low-cost alternatives to expensive learning programs?
5. What AI-driven insights help me optimize my education budget?
6. How does AI track promotions or discounts on learning resources?

AI for Categorizing Household Expenses

Scenario: An older adult wants to monitor household expenses, including cleaning, landscaping, and repairs.

Initial Question: "How can AI help me categorize and track my household expenses?"

Follow-on Questions:

1. What AI tools categorize household services like cleaning, landscaping, and maintenance?
2. Can AI compare my household expenses with similar-sized homes?
3. How does AI suggest budget-friendly alternatives for home services?
4. Can AI predict upcoming home-related costs based on my spending trends?
5. What AI-driven strategies help me optimize home service expenses?
6. How does AI analyze whether outsourcing or DIY home maintenance is more cost-effective?

AI for Charitable Contributions and Religious Donations

Scenario: A retiree wants to keep track of donations made to charities and religious organizations.

Initial Question: "How can AI help me manage and categorize my charitable contributions?"

Follow-on Questions:

1. What AI tools track and categorize charitable and religious donations?
2. Can AI suggest tax benefits associated with my charitable giving?
3. How does AI compare the financial impact of one-time versus recurring donations?
4. Can AI help me set a budget for future charitable contributions?
5. What AI-driven insights help me find reputable charities that align with my values?
6. How does AI track donation receipts for tax reporting?

AI for Managing Loan and Credit Card Payments

Scenario: A retiree wants to track and optimize their loan and credit card payments.

Initial Question: "How can AI help me categorize and manage my loan and credit card expenses?"

Follow-on Questions:

1. What AI tools categorize my loan and credit card payments separately?
2. Can AI track and predict interest payments over time?
3. How does AI compare different credit card rewards and fees?
4. Can AI suggest the best strategy for paying off loans efficiently?
5. What AI-driven alerts notify me when payments are due?
6. How does AI optimize loan refinancing or consolidation decisions?

Chapter 6: Financial Literacy Tools

AI-driven financial literacy platforms offer interactive tutorials on a range of topics, including taxes, investments, and credit management. These tools simplify complex financial concepts, ensuring older adults can make informed decisions without being overwhelmed by technical jargon.

AI chatbots and virtual assistants provide on-demand guidance, answering questions in real-time and recommending educational resources tailored to older adult learning styles. By improving financial literacy, AI empowers older adults to take greater control over their financial well-being.

This chapter provides a collection of **clear and insightful scenarios** designed to enhance your ability to interact effectively with ChatGPT regarding **Financial Literacy Tools**.

Each **scenario** is followed by:

- A carefully crafted **initial question** that prompts ChatGPT to analyze and respond thoughtfully to your scenario.
- A series of **follow-on questions** that demonstrate how to:
    - Refine your original inquiry for better results.
    - Seek clarification on ambiguous or complex responses.
    - Request additional details to deepen your understanding.

By following this approach, you will learn strategies to improve the **relevance and accuracy** of ChatGPT's responses, ensuring more **productive and meaningful conversations**.

Let's Get Started: How to Use This Chapter

1. **Find a Topic of Interest**
   - Scroll through the chapter and pick a "block" that interests you.
   - Each block includes a **title, scenario, initial question, and follow-on questions**.
   - You can start with any block—there's no required order.

2. **Start-up ChatGPT and Ask the AI a Question**
   - Copy-and-paste the **Initial Question** into ChatGPT's chat box or type your own question.
   - The **Initial Question** helps focus ChatGPT's response.

3. **Review of the AI's Response**
   - Read and analyze ChatGPT's answer.
   - Decide if you need more information.

4. **Ask the AI Follow-Up Questions**
   - Use some or all of the **Follow-On Questions** provided or ask your own questions.
   - More questions lead to deeper learning and better AI responses.

5. **Continue or Exit**
    - Keep exploring and refining your ChatGPT chat box inputs to improve the AI's response focus.
    - At any time, you can switch to another "block" of inquiry.
    - When you're done, simply exit the chat.
6. **The Goal of this Chapter and the Book**
    - Engage with ChatGPT as you would with a smart assistant to learn and improve how you use AI effectively!

AI for Understanding Personal Finance Basics

Scenario: A retiree wants to build a foundational understanding of personal finance.

Initial Question: "How can AI help me learn the basics of personal finance?"

Follow-on Questions:

1. What AI-driven platforms offer beginner-friendly financial education?
2. How does AI simplify complex financial terms for easy understanding?
3. Can AI personalize financial literacy lessons based on my experience level?
4. What AI-powered tools provide interactive tutorials on budgeting and saving?
5. How does AI recommend financial literacy resources tailored to my learning style?

6. Can AI track my progress in learning personal finance concepts?

AI for Learning About Credit Scores and Management

Scenario: An older adult wants to improve their credit score but doesn't know where to start.

Initial Question: "How can AI help me understand and improve my credit score?"

Follow-on Questions:

1. What AI tools analyze my credit report and suggest ways to boost my score?
2. How does AI explain factors that impact my credit score?
3. Can AI alert me to changes in my credit report and potential fraud?
4. What AI-driven strategies help manage debt and improve creditworthiness?
5. How does AI compare different credit cards based on rewards and fees?
6. Can AI predict how specific financial actions will affect my credit score?

AI for Understanding Investment Terminology

Scenario: A retiree is interested in investing but is unfamiliar with key financial terms.

Initial Question: "How can AI help me learn investment-related terminology?"

Follow-on Questions:

1. What AI-powered glossaries explain investment terms in simple language?
2. Can AI provide real-world examples of common investment strategies?
3. How does AI adapt explanations based on my financial literacy level?
4. What AI-driven tutorials break down stock market terminology?
5. How does AI differentiate between various types of investments, such as stocks, bonds, and ETFs?
6. Can AI quiz me on financial terms to reinforce my learning?

AI for Understanding Retirement Planning Concepts

Scenario: An older adult wants to understand key financial concepts related to retirement.

Initial Question: "How can AI help me learn about retirement planning?"

Follow-on Questions:

1. What AI-powered financial literacy tools explain retirement savings options?
2. How does AI simplify the differences between Roth and traditional IRAs?
3. Can AI predict my future retirement income based on different scenarios?

4. What AI-driven models explain Social Security benefits in a clear way?
5. How does AI compare annuities and other retirement income strategies?
6. Can AI provide interactive simulations to show different retirement outcomes?

AI for Learning About Taxes and Deductions

Scenario: A retiree wants to understand how taxes affect their financial situation.

Initial Question: "How can AI help me learn about tax deductions and strategies?"

Follow-on Questions:

1. What AI tools provide step-by-step explanations of tax deductions?
2. How does AI analyze my income sources to suggest tax-saving strategies?
3. Can AI simulate different tax scenarios to compare potential savings?
4. What AI-powered calculators estimate my tax liability in retirement?
5. How does AI explain tax implications for Social Security and pension withdrawals?
6. Can AI alert me to changes in tax laws that affect retirees?

AI for Understanding Debt Management Strategies

Scenario: An older adult wants to manage existing debt and avoid financial strain.

Initial Question: "How can AI help me develop a debt repayment strategy?"

Follow-on Questions:

1. What AI tools analyze my debt and suggest the best repayment method?
2. How does AI compare debt snowball and debt avalanche strategies?
3. Can AI recommend ways to reduce interest payments on outstanding debt?
4. What AI-driven alerts notify me of upcoming debt payments?
5. How does AI track my progress toward becoming debt-free?
6. Can AI suggest refinancing or consolidation options based on my financial profile?

AI for Understanding Inflation and Cost of Living Adjustments

Scenario: A retiree is worried about how inflation will affect their finances.

Initial Question: "How can AI help me understand and prepare for inflation?"

Follow-on Questions:

1. What AI tools analyze historical inflation trends and predict future changes?
2. How does AI track the impact of inflation on my personal budget?
3. Can AI suggest investment strategies to hedge against inflation?
4. What AI-driven insights help retirees adjust their spending habits?
5. How does AI compare cost-of-living adjustments across different locations?
6. Can AI provide personalized recommendations for preserving purchasing power?

AI for Learning About Passive Income Strategies

Scenario: A retiree wants to explore passive income options.

Initial Question: "How can AI help me learn about passive income opportunities?"

Follow-on Questions:

1. What AI-driven financial literacy tools explain different passive income streams?
2. How does AI compare rental income, dividends, and royalties?
3. Can AI analyze my financial situation and suggest passive income strategies?
4. What AI-powered insights help retirees build sustainable passive income?

5. How does AI track the performance of passive income investments?
6. Can AI simulate potential earnings from various passive income sources?

AI for Personalized Financial Literacy Courses

Scenario: A retiree wants a customized financial learning plan.

Initial Question: "How can AI create a personalized financial literacy learning plan for me?"

Follow-on Questions:

1. What AI tools assess my current financial knowledge and learning needs?
2. Can AI recommend specific courses based on my interests and goals?
3. How does AI adjust learning content as I progress?
4. What AI-driven quizzes evaluate my understanding of financial concepts?
5. How does AI integrate real-world financial scenarios into learning?
6. Can AI track my financial literacy improvement over time?

AI for Understanding Estate Planning and Wealth Transfer

Scenario: An older adult wants to understand how to pass on assets to their heirs.

Initial Question: "How can AI help me learn about estate planning and wealth transfer?"

Follow-on Questions:

1. What AI-powered financial literacy tools explain estate planning basics?
2. How does AI differentiate between wills, trusts, and other estate planning tools?
3. Can AI simulate different inheritance scenarios to show their impact?
4. What AI-driven insights help me minimize estate taxes?
5. How does AI integrate charitable giving into estate planning?
6. Can AI track legal changes that might affect my estate plan?

AI for Understanding Stock Market Trends

Scenario: A retiree wants to learn how the stock market works and how trends are identified.

Initial Question: "How can AI help me understand stock market trends?"

Follow-on Questions:

1. What AI-powered tools analyze stock market trends in real time?
2. How does AI predict market movements based on historical data?
3. Can AI explain key financial indicators like P/E ratios and earnings reports?
4. What AI-driven resources simplify technical stock market concepts?

5. How does AI compare different investment strategies for retirees?
6. Can AI provide simulated stock market trading to improve my learning?

AI for Understanding Cryptocurrency and Digital Assets

Scenario: A retiree is curious about cryptocurrency but unsure where to start.

Initial Question: "How can AI help me learn about cryptocurrency and digital assets?"

Follow-on Questions:

1. What AI-powered platforms provide beginner-friendly cryptocurrency education?
2. How does AI compare different cryptocurrencies based on risk and utility?
3. Can AI explain how blockchain technology works in simple terms?
4. What AI-driven insights help identify scams and fraudulent crypto investments?
5. How does AI track cryptocurrency price trends and volatility?
6. Can AI recommend safe platforms for buying and storing digital assets?

AI for Learning About Financial Scams and Fraud Prevention

Scenario: A retiree wants to recognize and avoid common financial scams.

Initial Question: "How can AI help me identify and protect myself from financial scams?"

Follow-on Questions:

1. What AI tools analyze emails and messages to detect phishing scams?
2. How does AI identify fraudulent investment schemes?
3. Can AI simulate real-world scam scenarios to improve awareness?
4. What AI-driven alerts notify me of emerging financial fraud tactics?
5. How does AI compare safe versus risky financial platforms?
6. Can AI provide personalized fraud prevention strategies based on my spending habits?

AI for Budgeting and Expense Tracking Education

Scenario: A retiree wants to understand how to create and manage a budget effectively.

Initial Question: "How can AI help me learn the principles of budgeting?"

Follow-on Questions:

1. What AI-driven budgeting tools offer interactive financial education?
2. How does AI categorize my expenses to identify spending patterns?
3. Can AI create a simulated budget based on different income levels?
4. What AI-powered alerts notify me when I exceed my budget?

5. How does AI compare different budgeting strategies for retirees?
6. Can AI integrate my financial goals into an automated budgeting plan?

AI for Understanding Insurance Policies and Coverage

Scenario: A retiree wants to learn about different types of insurance and how they work.

Initial Question: "How can AI help me understand my insurance coverage options?"

Follow-on Questions:

1. What AI-driven tools explain the differences between life, health, and home insurance?
2. How does AI compare insurance policies to find the best coverage for my needs?
3. Can AI analyze my financial situation and recommend optimal coverage levels?
4. What AI-powered alerts notify me of upcoming policy renewals?
5. How does AI track changes in insurance premiums over time?
6. Can AI simulate different scenarios to show how insurance benefits apply in real-life situations?

AI for Learning About Tax-Efficient Investment Strategies

Scenario: A retiree wants to minimize taxes on their investments while maximizing returns.

Initial Question: "How can AI help me understand tax-efficient investing?"

Follow-on Questions:

1. What AI-driven platforms explain how capital gains taxes impact investments?
2. How does AI compare tax-advantaged accounts like Roth IRAs and traditional IRAs?
3. Can AI recommend investment strategies that minimize tax liability?
4. What AI-powered simulations show the effects of different tax planning approaches?
5. How does AI predict the tax implications of withdrawing funds from retirement accounts?
6. Can AI suggest tax-efficient rebalancing strategies for my portfolio?

AI for Learning About Estate Planning and Inheritance Laws

Scenario: A retiree wants to ensure their estate is properly structured for inheritance.

Initial Question: "How can AI help me understand estate planning and inheritance laws?"

Follow-on Questions:

1. What AI tools simplify estate planning concepts for retirees?
2. How does AI compare wills, trusts, and beneficiary designations?
3. Can AI estimate potential estate taxes and recommend strategies to minimize them?

4. What AI-driven insights help ensure my assets are distributed according to my wishes?
5. How does AI track updates to inheritance laws that may affect my estate plan?
6. Can AI provide guidance on selecting an executor for my estate?

AI for Learning About Interest Rates and Loans

Scenario: A retiree wants to understand how interest rates impact loans and savings.

Initial Question: "How can AI help me understand how interest rates affect my finances?"

Follow-on Questions:

1. What AI-driven tools explain how interest rates impact loan payments?
2. How does AI compare fixed and variable interest rates?
3. Can AI analyze my loan terms and suggest refinancing options?
4. What AI-powered insights show the benefits of paying off loans early?
5. How does AI track Federal Reserve interest rate changes and their impact on savings?
6. Can AI predict how interest rate fluctuations will affect my financial planning?

AI for Learning About Real Estate Investment Strategies

Scenario: A retiree wants to explore real estate as an investment option.

Initial Question: "How can AI help me learn about real estate investing?"

Follow-on Questions:

1. What AI-driven platforms provide beginner-friendly real estate investment education?
2. How does AI analyze market trends to identify profitable real estate opportunities?
3. Can AI compare rental property income potential in different locations?
4. What AI-powered insights help manage real estate cash flow and expenses?
5. How does AI predict future property appreciation and depreciation?
6. Can AI recommend investment strategies based on my risk tolerance and financial goals?

AI for Understanding Compound Interest and Savings Growth

Scenario: A retiree wants to understand how compound interest works in savings and investments.

Initial Question: "How can AI help me understand the impact of compound interest?"

Follow-on Questions:

1. What AI-driven calculators show how compound interest affects long-term savings?
2. How does AI compare simple interest versus compound interest?
3. Can AI estimate future savings growth based on different deposit amounts?
4. What AI-powered simulations demonstrate the effects of starting to save early?
5. How does AI track changes in interest rates and their impact on savings?
6. Can AI recommend high-yield savings accounts or investment options that maximize compound interest?

Chapter 7: Tax Preparation

AI-driven tax preparation tools streamline the filing process by identifying potential deductions, optimizing tax credits, and ensuring accuracy. These systems analyze financial documents, cross-check entries for errors, and provide step-by-step guidance for tax compliance.

AI platforms may even integrate with tax authorities to facilitate direct filing, reducing the time and effort required for manual submissions. By automating tax preparation, older adults can avoid costly mistakes and maximize their returns with minimal stress.

This chapter provides a collection of **clear and insightful scenarios** designed to enhance your ability to interact effectively with ChatGPT regarding **Tax Preparation**.

Each **scenario** is followed by:

- A carefully crafted **initial question** that prompts ChatGPT to analyze and respond thoughtfully to your scenario.
- A series of **follow-on questions** that demonstrate how to:
    - Refine your original inquiry for better results.
    - Seek clarification on ambiguous or complex responses.
    - Request additional details to deepen your understanding.

By following this approach, you will learn strategies to improve the **relevance and accuracy** of ChatGPT's responses, ensuring more **productive and meaningful conversations**.

Let's Get Started: How to Use This Chapter

1. **Find a Topic of Interest**
   - Scroll through the chapter and pick a "block" that interests you.
   - Each block includes a **title, scenario, initial question, and follow-on questions**.
   - You can start with any block—there's no required order.

2. **Start-up ChatGPT and Ask the AI a Question**
   - Copy-and-paste the **Initial Question** into ChatGPT's chat box or type your own question.
   - The **Initial Question** helps focus ChatGPT's response.

3. **Review of the AI's Response**
   - Read and analyze ChatGPT's answer.
   - Decide if you need more information.

4. **Ask the AI Follow-Up Questions**
   - Use some or all of the **Follow-On Questions** provided or ask your own questions.
   - More questions lead to deeper learning and better AI responses.

5. **Continue or Exit**
   - Keep exploring and refining your ChatGPT chat box inputs to improve the AI's response focus.
   - At any time, you can switch to another "block" of inquiry.
   - When you're done, simply exit the chat.

6. **The Goal of this Chapter and the Book**
    - Engage with ChatGPT as you would with a smart assistant to learn and improve how you use AI effectively!

AI for Identifying Tax Deductions

Scenario: A retiree wants to maximize their tax deductions but isn't sure what qualifies.

Initial Question: "How can AI help me identify tax deductions I may be eligible for?"

Follow-on Questions:

1. What AI-powered tools analyze my financial records for eligible deductions?
2. How does AI differentiate between itemized and standard deductions?
3. Can AI suggest additional deductions based on my retirement status?
4. What AI-driven recommendations help me reduce taxable income legally?
5. How does AI track changes in tax laws that affect deduction eligibility?
6. Can AI simulate different deduction scenarios to maximize my tax savings?

AI for Optimizing Tax Credits

Scenario: A retiree wants to ensure they are claiming all available tax credits.

Initial Question: "How can AI help me determine which tax credits I qualify for?"

Follow-on Questions:

1. What AI-driven platforms analyze my financial history to find tax credits?
2. How does AI compare refundable and non-refundable tax credits?
3. Can AI predict the impact of tax credits on my overall return?
4. What AI tools track eligibility changes for older adult-specific tax credits?
5. How does AI integrate tax credit calculations with my total tax liability?
6. Can AI alert me to newly available tax credits I may not be aware of?

AI for Automating Tax Document Organization

Scenario: A retiree struggles with organizing tax-related documents each year.

Initial Question: "How can AI help me organize my tax documents efficiently?"

Follow-on Questions:

1. What AI tools categorize and store my financial records for tax season?
2. How does AI extract and summarize key information from receipts and statements?
3. Can AI generate an itemized report of my income and expenses for tax filing?
4. What AI-driven alerts remind me of missing or incomplete documents?
5. How does AI integrate with cloud storage to keep my records secure?
6. Can AI automate the retrieval of tax-related forms from my financial institutions?

AI for Estimating Tax Liability Before Filing

Scenario: A retiree wants to estimate the amount of money they will owe before filing.

Initial Question: "How can AI help me estimate my tax liability before filing?"

Follow-on Questions:

1. What AI-powered tax calculators provide an early estimate of taxes owed?
2. How does AI factor in income, deductions, and credits for accuracy?
3. Can AI predict how my tax liability changes under different filing statuses?
4. What AI-driven insights help me adjust my finances to lower my tax bill?

5. How does AI track estimated tax payments throughout the year?
6. Can AI compare previous years' tax liabilities to identify trends or issues?

AI for Detecting Tax Filing Errors

Scenario: A retiree is concerned about making mistakes on their tax return.

Initial Question: "How can AI help me detect and correct errors before filing my taxes?"

Follow-on Questions:

1. What AI tools review tax returns for common errors and inconsistencies?
2. How does AI cross-check data between financial documents and my tax return?
3. Can AI alert me to missing or incorrect information before submission?
4. What AI-driven insights help me avoid penalties related to filing mistakes?
5. How does AI ensure my tax return complies with the latest tax regulations?
6. Can AI compare my current tax return to previous filings for accuracy checks?

AI for Choosing Between Standard and Itemized Deductions

Scenario: A retiree is unsure whether to take the standard deduction or itemize.

Initial Question: "How can AI help me decide whether to take the standard deduction or itemize each deduction?"

Follow-on Questions:

1. What AI tools calculate the financial impact of each deduction method?
2. How does AI analyze my past expenses to determine potential tax savings?
3. Can AI compare deduction scenarios based on different income levels?
4. What AI-driven recommendations help retirees optimize their deductions?
5. How does AI track changes in standard deduction amounts each year?
6. Can AI suggest tax planning strategies based on my deduction choice?

AI for Managing Quarterly Estimated Taxes

Scenario: A retiree with investment income needs to manage estimated tax payments.

Initial Question: "How can AI help me calculate and manage quarterly estimated tax payments?"

Follow-on Questions:

1. What AI-powered tools estimate my quarterly tax payments?
2. How does AI track changes in income to adjust estimated taxes accordingly?
3. Can AI notify me of upcoming tax deadlines to avoid penalties?
4. What AI-driven insights help me optimize my estimated tax payments?
5. How does AI factor in deductions and credits when calculating quarterly payments?
6. Can AI automate tax payment reminders and processing?

AI for Understanding Tax Implications of Social Security Benefits

Scenario: A retiree wants to know if their Social Security income is taxable.

Initial Question: "How can AI help me understand the taxability of Social Security benefits?"

Follow-on Questions:

1. What AI tools calculate how much of my Social Security income is taxable?
2. How does AI integrate my other income sources to determine tax liability?
3. Can AI suggest strategies to minimize taxes on Social Security?
4. What AI-driven insights compare tax brackets for Social Security recipients?
5. How does AI track legislative changes affecting Social Security taxation?
6. Can AI simulate different withdrawal strategies to reduce tax burdens?

AI for Managing Tax Implications of Required Minimum Distributions (RMDs)

Scenario: A retiree needs guidance on RMDs from their retirement accounts.

Initial Question: "How can AI help me manage the tax impact of my required minimum distributions?"

Follow-on Questions:

1. What AI tools calculate my required minimum distributions each year?
2. How does AI predict the tax consequences of different RMD strategies?
3. Can AI compare the benefits of withdrawing only the RMD versus taking more?
4. What AI-driven insights help reduce taxes on RMDs through charitable giving?
5. How does AI track deadlines to avoid penalties for missed RMDs?
6. Can AI suggest reinvestment strategies to optimize RMD withdrawals?

AI for Filing Taxes Online with Minimal Effort

Scenario: A retiree wants to file taxes online but is unsure where to start.

Initial Question: "How can AI help me file my taxes online efficiently?"

Follow-on Questions:

1. What AI-powered tax platforms simplify the online filing process?
2. How does AI integrate with the IRS for direct e-filing?
3. Can AI automate data entry to reduce manual input errors?
4. What AI-driven insights help maximize my refund while ensuring compliance?
5. How does AI compare different online tax preparation services?
6. Can AI provide a step-by-step guide to filing my taxes with confidence?

AI for Comparing Different Tax Filing Statuses

Scenario: A retiree wants to understand how different tax filing statuses affect their return.

Initial Question: "How can AI help me determine the best tax filing status for my situation?"

Follow-on Questions:

1. What AI tools compare single, married, and head-of-household filing statuses?
2. How does AI estimate tax savings based on different filing statuses?
3. Can AI predict how my tax liability changes if my filing status changes?
4. What AI-driven recommendations help me optimize deductions based on my filing status?
5. How does AI factor in Social Security benefits and pension income when suggesting a filing status?

6. Can AI simulate future tax scenarios to help plan for life changes?

AI for Understanding Capital Gains Taxes

Scenario: A retiree that sold stocks wants to understand how capital gains taxes apply.

Initial Question: "How can AI help me calculate and minimize capital gains taxes?"

Follow-on Questions:

1. What AI tools calculate short-term versus long-term capital gains taxes?
2. How does AI track my investment history to determine cost basis?
3. Can AI suggest tax-efficient strategies for selling investments?
4. What AI-driven insights help me balance capital gains with losses for tax benefits?
5. How does AI predict the impact of capital gains on my total tax bill?
6. Can AI recommend timing strategies to reduce capital gains tax liability?

AI for Managing State vs. Federal Tax Differences

Scenario: A retiree who recently moved wants to understand state and federal tax differences.

Initial Question: "How can AI help me compare state and federal tax obligations?"

Follow-on Questions:

1. What AI tools analyze differences in state and federal tax laws?
2. How does AI estimate my total tax burden across multiple states?
3. Can AI suggest tax-friendly states for retirement based on my income sources?
4. What AI-driven insights help me understand how state tax laws affect Social Security and pension income?
5. How does AI track state tax credits and exemptions available to retirees?
6. Can AI provide a side-by-side comparison of state tax rates for my financial situation?

AI for Analyzing Tax Implications of Charitable Donations

Scenario: A retiree who donates regularly wants to understand tax benefits.

Initial Question: "How can AI help me optimize the tax benefits of my charitable donations?"

Follow-on Questions:

1. What AI tools track and categorize my charitable contributions for tax reporting?
2. How does AI differentiate between cash and non-cash donations for tax purposes?

3. Can AI estimate the amount of money I can deduct based on donation limits?
4. What AI-driven recommendations help me maximize the impact of charitable giving?
5. How does AI compare donor-advised funds with direct donations for tax benefits?
6. Can AI suggest tax-friendly ways to donate assets like stocks or real estate?

AI for Predicting Future Tax Brackets

Scenario: A retiree wants to estimate their tax bracket in future years.

Initial Question: "How can AI help me predict my future tax bracket?"

Follow-on Questions:

1. What AI tools analyze my income trends to estimate future tax brackets?
2. How does AI factor in inflation and cost-of-living adjustments?
3. Can AI compare how different income sources affect my tax bracket?
4. What AI-driven strategies help me plan withdrawals to stay in a lower bracket?
5. How does AI estimate the impact of RMDs and Social Security on future taxes?
6. Can AI suggest tax-efficient ways to shift income to lower-tax years?

AI for Managing Tax Implications of Home Sales

Scenario: A retiree who sold their home wants to understand capital gains tax implications.

Initial Question: "How can AI help me calculate and minimize taxes on my home sale?"

Follow-on Questions:

1. What AI tools estimate my home sale profit and potential tax liability?
2. How does AI determine whether I qualify for the home sale tax exclusion?
3. Can AI track home improvement costs to adjust my cost basis?
4. What AI-driven strategies help me defer or reduce capital gains taxes?
5. How does AI compare selling vs. renting out my home for tax efficiency?
6. Can AI predict how future property sales may impact my taxes?

AI for Understanding Required Minimum Distribution (RMD) Tax Implications

Scenario: A retiree must take RMDs and wants to manage tax consequences.

Initial Question: "How can AI help me manage taxes on required minimum distributions?"

Follow-on Questions:

1. What AI tools calculate my RMDs based on my account balances?
2. How does AI estimate the tax impact of different RMD withdrawal strategies?
3. Can AI suggest ways to offset RMD taxes, such as charitable distributions?
4. What AI-driven insights help me avoid penalties for missing RMD deadlines?
5. How does AI track RMD schedules across multiple retirement accounts?
6. Can AI optimize my RMD withdrawals to minimize their impact on my tax bracket?

AI for Managing Self-Employment Taxes in Retirement

Scenario: A retiree with freelance income wants to understand self-employment taxes.

Initial Question: "How can AI help me manage self-employment taxes in retirement?"

Follow-on Questions:

1. What AI tools estimate my self-employment tax liability?
2. How does AI track deductible business expenses to reduce taxable income?
3. Can AI compare self-employment tax obligations to regular payroll taxes?
4. What AI-driven recommendations help me optimize tax payments for freelance work?

5. How does AI integrate self-employment income into my overall retirement tax strategy?
6. Can AI suggest retirement accounts that offer tax benefits for self-employed retirees?

AI for Understanding Tax-Free Investment Options

Scenario: A retiree wants to explore tax-free investment opportunities.

Initial Question: "How can AI help me find tax-free investment options?"

Follow-on Questions:

1. What AI-driven tools analyze tax-free municipal bonds and their benefits?
2. How does AI compare Roth IRA vs. traditional IRA tax implications?
3. Can AI suggest low-tax or tax-free strategies for my retirement portfolio?
4. What AI insights track legislative changes affecting tax-advantaged accounts?
5. How does AI estimate tax savings from shifting taxable assets into tax-free accounts?
6. Can AI predict how tax-free investments will perform compared to taxable alternatives?

AI for Managing Inheritance and Estate Tax Planning

Scenario: A retiree wants to ensure their heirs pay minimal estate taxes.

Initial Question: "How can AI help me reduce estate and inheritance tax burdens?"

Follow-on Questions:

1. What AI tools estimate potential estate tax liabilities?
2. How does AI compare gifting strategies to reduce taxable estate value?
3. Can AI track estate tax exemption limits and recommend planning strategies?
4. What AI-driven insights help minimize inheritance taxes for beneficiaries?
5. How does AI compare different trust structures for estate planning?
6. Can AI predict how legislative changes may affect estate tax planning?

Chapter 8: Bill Payment Automation

Managing recurring bills can be challenging, but AI-powered automation tools simplify this process by tracking due dates and processing payments automatically. These systems send reminders for upcoming bills and notify users of insufficient funds, helping older adults avoid late fees and financial penalties.

By eliminating manual payment tasks, older adults can focus on other aspects of financial management while maintaining a strong credit history.

This chapter provides a collection of **clear and insightful scenarios** designed to enhance your ability to interact effectively with ChatGPT regarding **Bill Payment Automation**.

Each **scenario** is followed by:

- A carefully crafted **initial question** that prompts ChatGPT to analyze and respond thoughtfully to your scenario.
- A series of **follow-on questions** that demonstrate how to:
  - Refine your original inquiry for better results.
  - Seek clarification on ambiguous or complex responses.
  - Request additional details to deepen your understanding.

By following this approach, you will learn strategies to improve the **relevance and accuracy** of ChatGPT's responses, ensuring more **productive and meaningful conversations**.

Let's Get Started: How to Use This Chapter

1. **Find a Topic of Interest**
   - Scroll through the chapter and pick a "block" that interests you.
   - Each block includes a **title, scenario, initial question, and follow-on questions**.
   - You can start with any block—there's no required order.

2. **Start-up ChatGPT and Ask the AI a Question**
   - Copy-and-paste the **Initial Question** into ChatGPT's chat box or type your own question.
   - The **Initial Question** helps focus ChatGPT's response.

3. **Review of the AI's Response**
   - Read and analyze ChatGPT's answer.
   - Decide if you need more information.

4. **Ask the AI Follow-Up Questions**
   - Use some or all of the **Follow-On Questions** provided or ask your own questions.
   - More questions lead to deeper learning and better AI responses.

5. **Continue or Exit**
   - Keep exploring and refining your ChatGPT chat box inputs to improve the AI's response focus.
   - At any time, you can switch to another "block" of inquiry.
   - When you're done, simply exit the chat.

6. **The Goal of this Chapter and the Book**
   - Engage with ChatGPT as you would with a smart assistant to learn and improve how you use AI effectively!

AI for Automating Monthly Utility Payments

Scenario: A retiree wants to automate their electricity, water, and gas bill payments.

Initial Question: "How can AI help me automate my monthly-utility payments?"

Follow-on Questions:

1. What AI-powered tools track and schedule my recurring utility payments?
2. How does AI ensure my utility bills are paid on time?
3. Can AI notify me of any unexpected increases in my utility bills?
4. What AI-driven insights help me optimize my energy usage to reduce costs?
5. How does AI prevent overdraft fees when automating bill payments?
6. Can AI compare utility providers to suggest cost-effective alternatives?

AI for Tracking Subscription Services

Scenario: An older adult wants to automate subscription payments while avoiding unused services.

Initial Question: "How can AI help me track and automate my subscription payments?"

Follow-on Questions:

1. What AI tools categorize my active subscriptions and detect duplicate services?
2. Can AI cancel unwanted subscriptions to save money?
3. How does AI provide alerts before a free trial converts into a paid subscription?
4. What AI-driven insights compare similar subscription services for better pricing?
5. Can AI predict the amount of money I will spend on subscriptions over the next year?
6. How does AI ensure I never miss a subscription renewal payment?

AI for Avoiding Late Fees on Credit Card Payments

Scenario: A retiree wants to ensure they never miss a credit card payment.

Initial Question: "How can AI help me automate my credit card payments to avoid late fees?"

Follow-on Questions:

1. What AI-powered tools set up automatic credit card payments for minimum or full balance?
2. Can AI analyze my spending to recommend the best payment strategy?
3. How does AI notify me if my balance is too high before a payment is made?
4. What AI-driven alerts warn me if I am approaching my credit limit?
5. How does AI track multiple credit cards and optimize payment schedules?
6. Can AI help me automate debt reduction strategies for credit cards?

AI for Managing Property Tax Payments

Scenario: An older adult homeowner wants to ensure timely property tax payments.

Initial Question: "How can AI help me track and automate my property tax payments?"

Follow-on Questions:

1. What AI tools monitor my property tax deadlines and payment amounts?
2. Can AI compare different payment plans for property tax obligations?
3. How does AI track property tax deductions for filing during tax season?
4. What AI-driven alerts notify me of changes in my property tax rate?

5. Can AI ensure I don’t miss a payment due date to avoid penalties?
6. How does AI integrate property tax payments with my overall budget?

AI for Automating Medical Bill Payments

Scenario: A retiree with frequent medical expenses wants to ensure on-time payments.

Initial Question: "How can AI help me manage and automate my medical bill payments?"

Follow-on Questions:

1. What AI tools categorize and track my medical bills?
2. Can AI negotiate medical bills to reduce my out-of-pocket costs?
3. How does AI set up payment plans for large medical expenses?
4. What AI-driven reminders notify me of upcoming insurance premium payments?
5. Can AI predict my future medical expenses based on historical spending?
6. How does AI ensure my medical bills are processed correctly by my insurance?

AI for Handling Rent or Mortgage Payments

Scenario: A retiree wants to automate rent or mortgage payments while tracking housing costs.

Initial Question: "How can AI help me automate my rent or mortgage payments?"

Follow-on Questions:

1. What AI-powered tools ensure my rent or mortgage is paid on time each month?
2. Can AI notify me if my account balance is too low before the payment is processed?
3. How does AI track my total housing costs and suggest potential savings?
4. What AI-driven insights help compare refinancing options for a mortgage?
5. Can AI remind me when it's time to renew a lease or refinance my home?
6. How does AI prevent overpayment by verifying my rent or mortgage amount?

AI for Managing Insurance Premium Payments

Scenario: An older adult wants to automate payments for health, home, and auto insurance.

Initial Question: "How can AI help me track and automate my insurance premium payments?"

Follow-on Questions:

1. What AI tools ensure my insurance premiums are paid on time?
2. Can AI compare different insurance providers to find better rates?
3. How does AI track policy renewal dates and send reminders?

4. What AI-driven insights help optimize my insurance coverage?
5. Can AI notify me of discounts or policy changes that impact my payments?
6. How does AI ensure I never miss a payment that could result in coverage lapses?

AI for Managing Loan Repayments

Scenario: A retiree with a personal loan wants to automate repayments.

Initial Question: "How can AI help me automate my loan repayments?"

Follow-on Questions:

1. What AI-powered tools track my loan balances and ensure timely payments?
2. Can AI recommend extra payments to reduce interest costs?
3. How does AI notify me of opportunities to refinance my loan at a lower rate?
4. What AI-driven insights help me decide whether to pay off a loan early?
5. Can AI track my overall debt-to-income ratio and suggest improvements?
6. How does AI integrate my loan payments into my financial planning strategy?

AI for Handling Internet and Phone Bill Payments

Scenario: A retiree wants to automate and track their internet and phone bills.

Initial Question: "How can AI help me manage and automate my internet and phone bill payments?"

Follow-on Questions:

1. What AI tools ensure my telecom bills are paid automatically each month?
2. Can AI compare service providers to find better deals on internet and phone plans?
3. How does AI track my data usage and suggest more cost-effective plans?
4. What AI-driven alerts notify me of potential overcharges or billing errors?
5. Can AI remind me when the promotional pricing period is about to expire?
6. How does AI integrate these recurring payments into my budget?

AI for Detecting Unusual or Fraudulent Bill Payments

Scenario: A retiree wants to ensure all automated payments are legitimate.

Initial Question: "How can AI help me detect fraudulent or incorrect bill payments?"

Follow-on Questions:

1. What AI-powered tools monitor my transactions for suspicious activity?
2. Can AI flag unexpected increases in bill payments?
3. How does AI compare past bills to detect overcharges or fraudulent charges?
4. What AI-driven alerts notify me of duplicate or unauthorized payments?
5. Can AI automatically dispute a payment that appears fraudulent?
6. How does AI ensure my financial data remains secure when automating bill payments?

AI for Managing Household Maintenance Payments

Scenario: A retiree wants to automate payments for recurring home maintenance services, such as lawn care and housekeeping.

Initial Question: "How can AI help me automate and track my household maintenance payments?"

Follow-on Questions:

1. What AI-powered tools schedule and track home maintenance payments?
2. Can AI set reminders for upcoming service payments and contract renewals?
3. How does AI compare service providers to find cost-effective options?
4. What AI-driven alerts notify me if a service fee increases unexpectedly?

5. Can AI negotiate better rates with home maintenance providers?
6. How does AI integrate household maintenance expenses into my monthly budget?

AI for Coordinating Multiple Bill Due Dates

Scenario: A retiree wants to organize all their bill payments on the same date to simplify budgeting.

Initial Question: "How can AI help me align my bill due dates for easier financial management?"

Follow-on Questions:

1. What AI-powered tools allow me to adjust my bill due dates?
2. Can AI negotiate with service providers to change payment schedules?
3. How does AI track all my bill payments in one place?
4. What AI-driven insights help me plan cash flow around bill payments?
5. Can AI notify me if a new bill conflicts with my payment schedule?
6. How does AI ensure payments are made efficiently without overdrawing my account?

AI for Budgeting Bill Payments with Irregular Income

Scenario: A retiree with a fluctuating income wants to automate bill payments without overdrawing their account.

Initial Question: "How can AI help me automate bill payments while managing an irregular income?"

Follow-on Questions:

1. What AI tools predict income variations and adjust bill payments accordingly?
2. Can AI schedule payments based on cash flow forecasts?
3. How does AI prioritize which bills to pay first if funds are limited?
4. What AI-driven alerts notify me when my balance is too low for an upcoming bill?
5. Can AI create an emergency fund strategy for covering unexpected shortfalls?
6. How does AI analyze past income trends to recommend optimal budgeting plans?

AI for Handling One-Time and Annual Bill Payments

Scenario: A retiree wants to automate payments for bills that aren't monthly, such as annual insurance premiums.

Initial Question: "How can AI help me automate non-monthly bill payments?"

Follow-on Questions:

1. What AI tools track and remind me of upcoming annual or semi-annual payments?
2. Can AI create a savings plan to prepare for large annual expenses?
3. How does AI categorize and separate one-time versus recurring payments?

4. What AI-driven alerts notify me of bill payments due far enough in advance?
5. Can AI automate payments for tax bills, home warranties, or annual subscriptions?
6. How does AI optimize my cash flow for handling irregular bills without financial strain?

AI for Bill Payment Security and Fraud Prevention

Scenario: A retiree is concerned about the security of their automated bill payments.

Initial Question: "How can AI help ensure my automated bill payments are secure?"

Follow-on Questions:

1. What AI-powered tools detect unauthorized or fraudulent transactions?
2. Can AI flag suspicious payments before they are processed?
3. How does AI integrate with banks to provide extra layers of security?
4. What AI-driven alerts notify me of attempts to modify my payment information?
5. Can AI recommend secure payment platforms for bill automation?
6. How does AI protect my financial data from cyber threats?

AI for Managing Split Bill Payments

Scenario: A retiree who shares expenses with a spouse or family member wants to automate split payments.

Initial Question: "How can AI help me automate and track shared bill payments?"

Follow-on Questions:

1. What AI-powered tools allow for automated bill-splitting between multiple people?
2. Can AI ensure each party pays their fair share on time?
3. How does AI track who has paid what and send reminders if a payment is missing?
4. What AI-driven alerts notify me if a shared payment changes unexpectedly?
5. Can AI suggest fair ways to divide shared expenses over time?
6. How does AI integrate split payments with overall budgeting tools?

AI for Optimizing Payment Methods for Bills

Scenario: A retiree wants to ensure they are using the best payment methods for different bills.

Initial Question: "How can AI help me choose the best payment methods for my bills?"

Follow-on Questions:

1. What AI tools compare credit card, debit, and bank transfer options for bill payments?

2. Can AI recommend credit cards that maximize benefits for bill payments?
3. How does AI minimize transaction fees for automated bill payments?
4. What AI-driven insights help track cash back and discount opportunities?
5. Can AI alert me if a payment method is about to expire or become invalid?
6. How does AI suggest alternative payment strategies to reduce costs?

AI for Managing Unexpected Bill Increases

Scenario: A retiree notices that that bills may fluctuate unexpectedly and wants to track cost changes.

Initial Question: "How can AI help me detect and respond to sudden bill increases?"

Follow-on Questions:

1. What AI tools track and compare past and current bill amounts?
2. Can AI notify me when a bill increase exceeds my expected budget?
3. How does AI analyze the reason for cost fluctuations in my bills?
4. What AI-driven insights help negotiate better rates with service providers?
5. Can AI suggest alternative providers if a bill increase is unreasonable?
6. How does AI ensure I am only charged for services I actually use?

AI for Automating Travel and Vacation-Related Bills

Scenario: A retiree frequently travels and wants to ensure bill payments continue smoothly.

Initial Question: "How can AI help me manage my bills while traveling?"

Follow-on Questions:

1. What AI tools allow me to automate bill payments while I am away?
2. Can AI alert me if a payment issue arises while I'm traveling?
3. How does AI ensure scheduled payments, based on different time zones and banking hours, are made on time?
4. What AI-driven security measures protect against fraud when paying bills from abroad?
5. Can AI temporarily adjust payment limits or schedules based on my travel plans?
6. How does AI ensure I don't miss bills due to changes in internet or phone access?

AI for Managing Late Payment Notices and Fee Avoidance

Scenario: A retiree wants to avoid late payment fees and disputes for delayed bills.

Initial Question: "How can AI help me prevent and manage late bill payments?"

Follow-on Questions:

1. What AI-powered tools provide proactive alerts for due dates?
2. Can AI negotiate with service providers to waive late fees?
3. How does AI track and dispute incorrect late payment notices?
4. What AI-driven insights help me set up emergency payment options?
5. Can AI predict which payments I am most likely to miss and suggest solutions?
6. How does AI automate communication with service providers in case of delayed payments?

Chapter 9: Debt Management

AI tools can analyze an older adult's debt profile and develop customized repayment plans based on their financial situation. These platforms identify opportunities for consolidating loans, suggest priority repayment strategies, and provide insights into minimizing interest payments.

By automating debt tracking and providing real-time financial advice, AI empowers older adults to regain control over their finances and work toward financial independence.

This chapter provides a collection of **clear and insightful scenarios** designed to enhance your ability to interact effectively with ChatGPT regarding **Debt Management**.

Each **scenario** is followed by:

- A carefully crafted **initial question** that prompts ChatGPT to analyze and respond thoughtfully to your scenario.
- A series of **follow-on questions** that demonstrate how to:
    - Refine your original inquiry for better results.
    - Seek clarification on ambiguous or complex responses.
    - Request additional details to deepen your understanding.

By following this approach, you will learn strategies to improve the **relevance and accuracy** of ChatGPT's responses, ensuring more **productive and meaningful conversations**.

Let's Get Started: How to Use This Chapter

1. **Find a Topic of Interest**
   - Scroll through the chapter and pick a "block" that interests you.
   - Each block includes a **title, scenario, initial question, and follow-on questions**.
   - You can start with any block—there's no required order.
2. **Start-up ChatGPT and Ask the AI a Question**
   - Copy-and-paste the **Initial Question** into ChatGPT's chat box or type your own question.
   - The **Initial Question** helps focus ChatGPT's response.
3. **Review of the AI's Response**
   - Read and analyze ChatGPT's answer.
   - Decide if you need more information.
4. **Ask the AI Follow-Up Questions**
   - Use some or all of the **Follow-On Questions** provided or ask your own questions.
   - More questions lead to deeper learning and better AI responses.
5. **Continue or Exit**
   - Keep exploring and refining your ChatGPT chat box inputs to improve the AI's response focus.
   - At any time, you can switch to another "block" of inquiry.
   - When you're done, simply exit the chat.

6. **The Goal of this Chapter and the Book**
    - Engage with ChatGPT as you would with a smart assistant to learn and improve how you use AI effectively!

AI for Creating a Personalized Debt Repayment Plan

Scenario: A retiree wants to create a structured plan to pay off their outstanding debts.

Initial Question: "How can AI help me create a customized debt repayment plan?"

Follow-on Questions:

1. What AI tools analyze my debt and suggest the best repayment strategy?
2. Can AI prioritize my debts based on interest rates and balances?
3. How does AI compare the debt snowball vs. debt avalanche method?
4. What AI-driven insights help me allocate funds for debt while maintaining savings?
5. Can AI track my progress and suggest adjustments to my repayment plan?
6. How does AI ensure I stay on schedule with my debt payments?

AI for Identifying High-Interest Debt

Scenario: A retiree wants to pinpoint which debts are costing them the most in interest.

Initial Question: "How can AI help me identify my highest-interest debts?"

Follow-on Questions:

1. What AI tools analyze my debt profile and rank debts by interest cost?
2. Can AI estimate the amount of interest I will pay over a period of time on each debt?
3. How does AI compare different repayment strategies for high-interest debt?
4. What AI-driven alerts notify me if my interest rates increase?
5. Can AI recommend ways to negotiate lower interest rates?
6. How does AI track my interest payments and suggest cost-saving options?

AI for Automating Monthly Debt Payments

Scenario: An older adult wants to automate their debt repayments to avoid late fees.

Initial Question: "How can AI help me automate my debt payments?"

Follow-on Questions:

1. What AI-powered tools ensure my debt payments are made on time?
2. Can AI schedule automatic minimum payments to prevent missed deadlines?
3. How does AI notify me before payments are withdrawn from my account?

4. What AI-driven insights help me decide whether to pay more than the minimum?
5. Can AI optimize my payment schedule to align with my income cycle?
6. How does AI track my remaining balances and projected payoff dates?

AI for Negotiating Lower Interest Rates

Scenario: A retiree wants to reduce interest rates on their existing loans.

Initial Question: "How can AI help me negotiate lower interest rates on my debt?"

Follow-on Questions:

1. What AI tools analyze my credit profile and suggest rate negotiation strategies?
2. Can AI identify lenders that offer lower interest refinancing options?
3. How does AI track interest rate trends to find the best time for renegotiation?
4. What AI-driven insights help me improve my credit score to qualify for better rates?
5. Can AI draft negotiation letters to send to my lenders?
6. How does AI estimate my potential savings if I secure a lower interest rate?

AI for Managing Credit Card Debt

Scenario: An older adult wants to eliminate their credit card debt efficiently.

Initial Question: "How can AI help me reduce my credit card debt?"

Follow-on Questions:

1. What AI tools track my credit card balances and payment history?
2. Can AI recommend the best strategy for paying off multiple credit cards?
3. How does AI suggest balance transfer options to reduce interest costs?
4. What AI-driven alerts notify me of upcoming due dates and fees?
5. Can AI analyze my spending habits and suggest ways to minimize credit card use?
6. How does AI predict the long-term impact of paying more than the minimum payment?

AI for Debt Consolidation Recommendations

Scenario: A retiree wants to consolidate multiple loans into a single payment.

Initial Question: "How can AI help me determine if debt consolidation is a good option?"

Follow-on Questions:

1. What AI-powered tools compare different debt consolidation options?
2. Can AI calculate my potential savings from consolidating my debts?
3. How does AI identify lenders with favorable consolidation loan terms?
4. What AI-driven insights help me determine if consolidation improves my financial situation?
5. Can AI track my progress after consolidating my debts?
6. How does AI compare debt consolidation with other repayment strategies?

AI for Managing Medical Debt

Scenario: A retiree has accumulated medical debt and needs an efficient repayment plan.

Initial Question: "How can AI help me manage and pay off my medical debt?"

Follow-on Questions:

1. What AI tools categorize and prioritize my medical bills?
2. Can AI suggest payment plans or financial assistance options?
3. How does AI track billing errors or overcharges in my medical expenses?
4. What AI-driven insights help me negotiate with healthcare providers?
5. Can AI compare different medical financing options?
6. How does AI integrate medical debt into my overall debt repayment plan?

AI for Avoiding Debt Collection Issues

Scenario: A retiree wants to avoid debt collection problems and improve their financial standing.

Initial Question: "How can AI help me prevent and manage debt collection issues?"

Follow-on Questions:

1. What AI tools track and notify me of overdue accounts?
2. Can AI analyze debt collection notices and suggest responses?
3. How does AI protect me from fraudulent debt collection scams?
4. What AI-driven insights help me negotiate settlements with creditors?
5. Can AI automate communication with debt collectors to prevent harassment?
6. How does AI ensure my credit score is not impacted by collections unnecessarily?

AI for Debt-to-Income Ratio Analysis

Scenario: A retiree wants to understand how their debt compares to their income.

Initial Question: "How can AI help me analyze my debt-to-income ratio?"

Follow-on Questions:

1. What AI-powered tools calculate my debt-to-income ratio in real time?

2. Can AI track how my debt ratio changes as I make payments?
3. How does AI compare my ratio to financial stability benchmarks?
4. What AI-driven insights suggest ways to lower my debt ratio?
5. Can AI simulate different financial scenarios to improve my debt profile?
6. How does AI predict how my debt-to-income ratio will affect future credit applications?

AI for Tracking and Improving Credit Score While Paying Debt

Scenario: A retiree wants to monitor their credit score while repaying debt.

Initial Question: "How can AI help me track and improve my credit score while managing debt?"

Follow-on Questions:

1. What AI tools analyze how my debt payments affect my credit score?
2. Can AI suggest strategies to improve my score while reducing debt?
3. How does AI predict the impact of new credit applications on my score?
4. What AI-driven alerts notify me of negative credit report changes?
5. Can AI recommend the best credit-building financial habits?
6. How does AI ensure I maintain a strong credit profile while paying off debt?

AI for Predicting Future Debt Obligations

Scenario: A retiree wants to forecast future debt obligations based on their current financial status.

Initial Question: "How can AI help me predict and plan for future debt obligations?"

Follow-on Questions:

1. What AI tools analyze my debt trends and predict future liabilities?
2. Can AI estimate how long it will take to become debt-free?
3. How does AI track interest rate changes and their impact on future debt payments?
4. What AI-driven insights suggest adjustments to avoid financial strain?
5. Can AI simulate different repayment scenarios based on income changes?
6. How does AI integrate inflation into my long-term debt repayment plan?

AI for Automating Extra Debt Payments

Scenario: An older adult wants to make extra payments toward their debts without disrupting their budget.

Initial Question: "How can AI help me automate extra payments toward my debt?"

Follow-on Questions:

1. What AI-powered tools analyze my income and expenses to find surplus funds?
2. Can AI automatically allocate extra payments to the highest-interest debt?
3. How does AI track my remaining balances and suggest optimal payment adjustments?
4. What AI-driven insights prevent me from overcommitting extra payments?
5. Can AI adjust extra payments dynamically based on my financial situation?
6. How does AI compare the impact of small, frequent extra payments versus lump sums?

AI for Managing Co-Signed Loans and Shared Debt

Scenario: A retiree has co-signed a loan for a family member and wants to track it efficiently.

Initial Question: "How can AI help me monitor and manage a co-signed loan?"

Follow-on Questions:

1. What AI tools track the payment history of a co-signed loan?
2. Can AI notify me if a payment is missed on the loan I co-signed?
3. How does AI calculate the potential risk of a co-signed loan affecting my credit?
4. What AI-driven alerts notify me of changes in the loan terms or interest rate?

5. Can AI recommend strategies to remove myself as a co-signer?
6. How does AI predict how co-signed debt impacts my financial stability?

AI for Understanding and Negotiating Debt Settlement

Scenario: A retiree is struggling with debt and wants to explore settlement options.

Initial Question: "How can AI help me evaluate and negotiate debt settlement?"

Follow-on Questions:

1. What AI-powered tools analyze my debt to determine if settlement is a viable option?
2. Can AI estimate the amount of money I might save through debt settlement?
3. How does AI compare debt settlement with bankruptcy or consolidation?
4. What AI-driven insights help me negotiate with creditors for reduced payments?
5. Can AI automate communications with creditors to streamline the settlement process?
6. How does AI track my progress and ensure compliance with a settlement agreement?

AI for Identifying and Avoiding Predatory Lending

Scenario: A retiree wants to borrow money but is worried about falling into a predatory loan trap.

Initial Question: "How can AI help me identify and avoid predatory lending practices?"

Follow-on Questions:

1. What AI tools analyze loan terms for red flags?
2. Can AI compare interest rates and fees across multiple lenders?
3. How does AI detect hidden fees and aggressive loan terms?
4. What AI-driven alerts notify me if a lender is flagged for unethical practices?
5. Can AI recommend safer loan alternatives based on my financial needs?
6. How does AI track my loan agreements to ensure fair treatment?

AI for Managing Student Loan Debt in Retirement

Scenario: A retiree still has student loan debt and wants to manage payments efficiently.

Initial Question: "How can AI help me manage and pay off my student loans in retirement?"

Follow-on Questions:

1. What AI tools track my remaining student loan balance and payment schedule?

2. Can AI compare federal and private loan repayment options for retirees?
3. How does AI suggest income-driven repayment plans for older adults?
4. What AI-driven alerts notify me of loan forgiveness programs?
5. Can AI estimate how paying off my student loans affects my overall retirement plan?
6. How does AI help me refinance student loans to lower interest rates?

AI for Tracking Debt Across Multiple Financial Institutions

Scenario: A retiree has debt across multiple banks and wants a consolidated view.

Initial Question: "How can AI help me track and manage debt across multiple financial institutions?"

Follow-on Questions:

1. What AI-powered tools aggregate my debts into a single dashboard?
2. Can AI provide an overview of total debt, interest rates, and payment due dates?
3. How does AI suggest the most efficient way to allocate payments across institutions?
4. What AI-driven alerts notify me of changes in my debt terms from different lenders?
5. Can AI help me consolidate my debts to simplify management?
6. How does AI track automatic payments to ensure no duplicate payments occur?

AI for Understanding the Impact of Debt on Credit Scores

Scenario: A retiree wants to see how different debt management strategies affect their credit score.

Initial Question: "How can AI help me understand how debt affects my credit score?"

Follow-on Questions:

1. What AI tools analyze my credit report to track debt impact?
2. Can AI simulate how my credit score changes if I pay off certain debts first?
3. How does AI track my credit utilization ratio and suggest improvements?
4. What AI-driven insights help me rebuild my credit while repaying debt?
5. Can AI compare the long-term credit impact of debt consolidation versus full repayment?
6. How does AI provide personalized credit improvement recommendations based on my debt profile?

AI for Planning Debt Reduction Without Sacrificing Savings

Scenario: A retiree wants to pay off debt without depleting their retirement savings.

Initial Question: "How can AI help me reduce debt while maintaining my savings?"

Follow-on Questions:

1. What AI-powered tools balance debt repayment and savings contributions?
2. Can AI predict how different debt reduction strategies affect my future finances?
3. How does AI ensure I keep an emergency fund while paying off debt?
4. What AI-driven insights help me determine when to focus on debt vs. savings?
5. Can AI suggest tax-efficient ways to withdraw retirement funds for debt repayment?
6. How does AI track my financial goals to ensure both debt reduction and financial security?

AI for Helping Older Adults Avoid Debt in Retirement

Scenario: A retiree wants to prevent accumulating new debt while living on a fixed income.

Initial Question: "How can AI help me avoid taking on new debt in retirement?"

Follow-on Questions:

1. What AI-powered budgeting tools help me stay within my means?
2. Can AI track my expenses and suggest adjustments to prevent reliance on credit?
3. How does AI compare alternative income sources to avoid borrowing?
4. What AI-driven alerts notify me if I'm spending beyond my retirement budget?

5. Can AI recommend financial strategies that manage emergencies without using credit?
6. How does AI track my debt-free progress and suggest long-term financial habits?

Chapter 10: Legacy Planning

Estate planning is a critical aspect of financial management, and AI tools simplify this process by organizing wills, trusts, and beneficiary details. These systems provide checklists and legal guidance to ensure older adults' estate plans align with their wishes.

AI-powered platforms may also assist with tax-efficient estate planning, minimizing liabilities for beneficiaries. By leveraging AI for legacy planning, older adults can ensure their wealth is distributed according to their intentions while reducing stress for their loved ones.

This chapter provides a collection of **clear and insightful scenarios** designed to enhance your ability to interact effectively with ChatGPT regarding **Legacy Planning**.

Each **scenario** is followed by:

- A carefully crafted **initial question** that prompts ChatGPT to analyze and respond thoughtfully to your scenario.
- A series of **follow-on questions** that demonstrate how to:
    - Refine your original inquiry for better results.
    - Seek clarification on ambiguous or complex responses.
    - Request additional details to deepen your understanding.

By following this approach, you will learn strategies to improve the **relevance and accuracy** of ChatGPT's responses, ensuring more **productive and meaningful conversations**.

Let’s Get Started: How to Use This Chapter

1. **Find a Topic of Interest**
    - Scroll through the chapter and pick a “block” that interests you.
    - Each block includes a **title, scenario, initial question, and follow-on questions**.
    - You can start with any block—there’s no required order.

2. **Start-up ChatGPT and Ask the AI a Question**
    - Copy-and-paste the **Initial Question** into ChatGPT’s chat box or type your own question.
    - The **Initial Question** helps focus ChatGPT’s response.

3. **Review of the AI’s Response**
    - Read and analyze ChatGPT’s answer.
    - Decide if you need more information.

4. **Ask the AI Follow-Up Questions**
    - Use some or all of the **Follow-On Questions** provided or ask your own questions.
    - More questions lead to deeper learning and better AI responses.

5. **Continue or Exit**
    - Keep exploring and refining your ChatGPT chat box inputs to improve the AI’s response focus.
    - At any time, you can switch to another “block” of inquiry.
    - When you're done, simply exit the chat.

6. **The Goal of this Chapter and the Book**

    - Engage with ChatGPT as you would with a smart assistant to learn and improve how you use AI effectively!

AI for Organizing Estate Planning Documents

Scenario: A retiree wants to ensure all estate planning documents are in order.

Initial Question: "How can AI help me organize my estate planning documents?"

Follow-on Questions:

1. What AI-powered tools help track and store a retiree's will, trust, and beneficiary designations?
2. Can AI generate a checklist of essential estate planning documents?
3. How does AI ensure my estate plan complies with state and federal laws?
4. What AI-driven alerts notify me if documents need updating?
5. Can AI integrate with my financial accounts to ensure accurate asset distribution?
6. How does AI help me securely share my estate plan with my executor and heirs?

AI for Creating a Will

Scenario: An older adult wants to draft a will but is unsure where to start.

Initial Question: "How can AI help me create a legally valid will?"

Follow-on Questions:

1. What AI-powered platforms guide me through drafting a will?
2. Can AI suggest ways to structure my will to align with my intentions?
3. How does AI identify potential legal pitfalls in my estate plan?
4. What AI-driven insights help me ensure my assets are distributed fairly?
5. Can AI update my will as my financial situation changes?
6. How does AI integrate my will with other estate planning documents?

AI for Setting Up a Trust

Scenario: A retiree wants to establish an estate trust for their heirs.

Initial Question: "How can AI help me determine if a trust is right for my estate plan?"

Follow-on Questions:

1. What AI-powered tools analyze my estate and suggest appropriate trust structures?
2. Can AI compare revocable and irrevocable trusts for my situation?

3. How does AI optimize trust distribution to minimize tax liabilities?
4. What AI-driven insights help me select a trustee?
5. Can AI track changes in estate laws that impact my trust?
6. How does AI integrate my trust with my overall financial plan?

AI for Reducing Estate Taxes

Scenario: A retiree wants to minimize estate taxes for their heirs.

Initial Question: "How can AI help me develop a tax-efficient estate plan?"

Follow-on Questions:

1. What AI tools estimate my estate tax liabilities?
2. Can AI suggest gifting strategies to reduce taxable assets?
3. How does AI compare different estate planning techniques to lower taxes?
4. What AI-driven insights help ensure my heirs inherit tax-efficiently?
5. Can AI predict changes in tax laws that may affect my estate plan?
6. How does AI integrate tax-saving strategies into my estate distribution plan?

AI for Managing Beneficiary Designations

Scenario: An older adult wants to ensure all beneficiary designations are up to date.

Initial Question: "How can AI help me review and update my beneficiary designations?"

Follow-on Questions:

1. What AI-powered tools track all my financial accounts and their designated beneficiaries?
2. Can AI notify me if a beneficiary designation is missing or outdated?
3. How does AI ensure consistency between my will and beneficiary designations?
4. What AI-driven insights help me decide on contingent beneficiaries?
5. Can AI alert me to legal changes affecting beneficiary rules?
6. How does AI integrate beneficiary updates with my broader estate plan?

AI for Charitable Giving and Legacy Contributions

Scenario: A retiree wants to include charitable donations in their estate plan.

Initial Question: "How can AI help me structure charitable giving in my estate plan?"

Follow-on Questions:

1. What AI tools identify tax-efficient ways to donate assets to charity?
2. Can AI compare donor-advised funds vs. direct donations?
3. How does AI ensure my charitable contributions align with my values?
4. What AI-driven insights help maximize tax deductions for charitable giving?

5. Can AI track and document all my past and future charitable donations?
6. How does AI integrate charitable giving into my estate distribution plan?

AI for Ensuring Digital Asset Inheritance

Scenario: An older adult wants to make sure their digital assets are passed down properly.

Initial Question: "How can AI help me organize and transfer my digital assets to my heirs?"

Follow-on Questions:

1. What AI-powered tools help track my digital assets, such as passwords and online accounts?
2. Can AI ensure my digital assets comply with inheritance laws?
3. How does AI store and secure sensitive digital account information?
4. What AI-driven alerts notify me of changes in digital inheritance policies?
5. Can AI generate a digital estate plan to share with my executor?
6. How does AI integrate digital assets with my overall estate plan?

AI for Establishing Estate Fraud Protection

Scenario: A retiree wants to prevent unauthorized changes to their estate plan.

Initial Question: "How can AI help me protect my estate plan from fraud and manipulation?"

Follow-on Questions:

1. What AI tools detect suspicious activity related to my estate documents?
2. Can AI alert me if someone tries to alter my will or trust fraudulently?
3. How does AI compare my estate documents to prevent inconsistencies?
4. What AI-driven insights help me choose trustworthy executors and trustees?
5. Can AI verify the authenticity of witnesses and signatures?
6. How does AI track legal disputes that could affect my estate plan?

AI for Planning Business Succession

Scenario: An older adult business owner wants to ensure a smooth transition of their company.

Initial Question: "How can AI help me develop a business succession plan?"

Follow-on Questions:

1. What AI-powered tools analyze my business structure for succession planning?
2. Can AI recommend succession strategies that minimize tax liabilities?
3. How does AI compare selling vs. passing down my business to family?

4. What AI-driven insights help ensure a seamless leadership transition?
5. Can AI track changes in business inheritance laws?
6. How does AI integrate my business succession plan with my personal estate plan?

AI for Creating a Legacy Letter or Ethical Will

Scenario: A retiree wants to leave a personal message alongside their legal will.

Initial Question: "How can AI help me draft a legacy letter or ethical will?"

Follow-on Questions:

1. What AI tools guide me through writing a heartfelt legacy letter?
2. Can AI suggest themes and topics to include in my ethical will?
3. How does AI ensure my legacy letter complements my legal will?
4. What AI-driven insights help me craft a meaningful message for my heirs?
5. Can AI store and deliver my legacy letter at a future date?
6. How does AI integrate personal values and family history into my legacy planning?

AI for Planning Multi-Generational Wealth Transfer

Scenario: A retiree wants to ensure their wealth benefits multiple generations of their family.

Initial Question: "How can AI help me create a multi-generational wealth transfer strategy?"

Follow-on Questions:

1. What AI-powered tools assist in structuring a financial legacy for future generations?
2. Can AI recommend tax-efficient ways to pass down wealth to my children and grandchildren?
3. How does AI track changes in inheritance laws that affect multi-generational wealth transfer?
4. What AI-driven insights help balance fairness among multiple heirs?
5. Can AI simulate different inheritance scenarios to evaluate their long-term impact?
6. How does AI integrate education funds and trusts into a long-term legacy plan?

AI for Managing Life Insurance and Estate Integration

Scenario: An older adult wants to ensure their life insurance aligns with their estate plan.

Initial Question: "How can AI help me integrate my life insurance into my estate plan?"

Follow-on Questions:

1. What AI tools analyze my life insurance policies for estate planning purposes?
2. Can AI suggest whether my estate heirs should receive a lump sum or a structured payout?
3. How does AI track changes in insurance policies and estate tax laws?
4. What AI-driven insights help ensure my beneficiaries receive the maximum benefit?
5. Can AI predict the tax impact of different life insurance payout structures?
6. How does AI compare different life insurance options for estate planning purposes?

AI for Identifying Unclaimed Assets and Missing Accounts

Scenario: A retiree wants to locate and reclaim any forgotten financial accounts.

Initial Question: "How can AI help me identify and recover unclaimed assets?"

Follow-on Questions:

1. What AI-powered tools scan financial records for unclaimed assets?
2. Can AI check government databases for lost accounts or unclaimed funds?
3. How does AI verify whether old bank accounts, pensions, or stocks remain active?
4. What AI-driven alerts notify me of missing beneficiary designations?

5. Can AI track down forgotten real estate or investments from past decades?
6. How does AI integrate recovered assets into my estate plan?

AI for Preventing Family Disputes Over Inheritance

Scenario: An older adult wants to avoid conflicts between heirs over their estate.

Initial Question: "How can AI help me structure my estate plan to prevent family disputes?"

Follow-on Questions:

1. What AI-powered tools analyze my estate distribution for potential conflicts?
2. Can AI suggest ways to balance fairness among heirs?
3. How does AI compare inheritance structures that minimize legal disputes?
4. What AI-driven insights help me create a dispute resolution plan in my will?
5. Can AI track legal cases involving inheritance disputes for best practices?
6. How does AI document and clarify my intentions to ensure a smooth transition?

AI for Estate Planning with Blended Families

Scenario: A retiree with stepchildren and multiple marriages wants to ensure fair inheritance distribution.

Initial Question: "How can AI help me create an estate plan that accounts for my blended family?"

Follow-on Questions:

1. What AI-powered tools suggest estate planning strategies for blended families?
2. Can AI recommend ways to provide for both biological and stepchildren equitably?
3. How does AI analyze potential legal conflicts in a blended family estate plan?
4. What AI-driven insights help me balance spousal inheritance with children's interests?
5. Can AI track changing family dynamics and suggest necessary estate updates?
6. How does AI ensure my blended family estate plan remains legally sound and enforceable?

AI for Managing International Estate Planning

Scenario: A retiree with assets in multiple countries wants to simplify inheritance logistics.

Initial Question: "How can AI help me manage estate planning across multiple countries?"

Follow-on Questions:

1. What AI-powered tools track tax laws and inheritance regulations across different countries?
2. Can AI recommend ways to minimize cross-border estate taxation?

3. How does AI compare different legal frameworks for distributing international assets?
4. What AI-driven insights do heirs need to gain easy access to foreign-held assets?
5. Can AI automate compliance checks for multiple jurisdictions?
6. How does AI integrate international trusts and wills for seamless estate planning?

AI for Managing Philanthropic Legacy and Foundations

Scenario: A retiree wants to establish a foundation for long-term charitable giving.

Initial Question: "How can AI help me structure a philanthropic legacy or charitable foundation?"

Follow-on Questions:

1. What AI tools help me create a legally sound charitable foundation?
2. Can AI recommend tax-advantaged ways to fund charitable giving?
3. How does AI track and evaluate the impact of my philanthropic efforts?
4. What AI-driven insights help manage foundation spending and longevity?
5. Can AI ensure my foundation aligns with my values and long-term goals?
6. How does AI automate compliance and reporting requirements for charitable foundations?

AI for Handling Digital Inheritance and Social Media Accounts

Scenario: A retiree wants to manage their digital presence after they pass away.

Initial Question: "How can AI help me manage my digital inheritance and online accounts?"

Follow-on Questions:

1. What AI-powered tools track and store login information for heirs?
2. Can AI suggest best practices for managing social media accounts posthumously?
3. How does AI ensure digital assets like cryptocurrencies are passed down securely?
4. What AI-driven alerts notify me of changes in digital inheritance laws?
5. Can AI automate the closure or memorialization of online profiles?
6. How does AI integrate digital assets with my overall estate plan?

AI for Reviewing and Updating Estate Plans Over Time

Scenario: A retiree wants to keep their estate plan up to date as life changes.

Initial Question: "How can AI help me review and update my estate plan as needed?"

Follow-on Questions:

1. What AI tools track changes in my financial and family situation to suggest updates?
2. Can AI compare my current estate plan with my latest financial records?
3. How does AI alert me to legal changes that require an update to my estate documents?
4. What AI-driven insights help me determine when to revise my will or trust?
5. Can AI notify my attorney and financial advisor of necessary estate updates?
6. How does AI ensure my estate plan remains aligned with my goals and current laws?

AI for Automating Communication with Heirs and Executors

Scenario: A retiree wants to ensure their heirs and executor understand their estate plan.

Initial Question: "How can AI help me automate communication with my heirs and executor?"

Follow-on Questions:

1. What AI-powered tools provide heirs with access to relevant estate documents?
2. Can AI schedule automatic messages to be sent to heirs at key moments?
3. How does AI ensure my executor has clear guidance on managing my estate?
4. What AI-driven insights help me create a transparent inheritance process?

5. Can AI track and log any changes in my estate plan for future reference?
6. How does AI integrate legal and financial advisors into estate planning communications?

Made in the USA
Monee, IL
12 November 2026

9c2ce437-1207-4e64-8baa-9b0ebbf73e66R01